Dr Strangelove, I Presume

Dr Strangelove, I Presume

MICHAEL FOOT

VICTOR GOLLANCZ

LONDON

First published in Great Britain 1999
by Victor Gollancz
An imprint of the Cassell Group
Wellington House, 125 Strand, London WC2R 0BB

A catalogue record for this book is
available from the British Library.

ISBN 0 575 06693 8

Typeset by Rowland Phototypesetting Ltd,
Bury St Edmunds, Suffolk
Printed in Great Britain by
St Edmundsbury Press Ltd, Bury St Edmunds, Suffolk

2 4 6 8 9 7 5 3 1

Inscription

Inscriptions of this character are not always as carefully read as they should be, as I discovered when I wrote mine for my last book *HG: The History of Mr Wells*. My main point then was to express my indispensable debt to Una Cooze, which I renew now even more fervently. However, the other point was to stress that all errors or misjudgements in that volume should be laid at the door of V. S. Pritchett, who had so kindly encouraged me to proceed with that book at a meeting in his house on 10 July 1992. All the people who complained to me about that volume, both privately and in public, had misread the inscription as if there were a *not* in the wrong place. This time I have no such excuse or alibi. For my one-volume life of Aneurin Bevan published last year by Victor Gollancz, Brian Brivati wrote a brilliant introduction, which greatly added to the value of the book. This time he has assisted by reading an earlier draft of what I proposed. I must also eagerly acknowledge how much I owe to those who have sustained the work of the Campaign for Nuclear Disarmament, headed by Sheila Jones at the CND offices and William Peden in the House of Commons. All remaining errors, misjudgements *et al.* are my own and nobody else's. This last warning applies, even though the book has been read by such a brilliant copy-editor as Gillian Bromley. She has saved me from countless mistakes and follies for which I am grateful, but all outstanding ones remain my own.

NB: Again, all complaints about the H. G. Wells book should be sent to Victor Pritchett.

To Jill

All my previous books since 1945 have been dedicated to her, but this one especially. She was the most passionate CNDer of the lot, who saw from the start that man's invention of radioactive tortures for the future was the worst ever invasion of women's rights.

To the electors of

Devonport, Plymouth, and Ebbw Vale and Blaenau Gwent, who sent me to the House of Commons to speak freely on this subject and a few others, whatever the whips might say.

Contents

An open letter to Mr Vajpayee on Hiroshima Day, 1998

Sir

I am writing on behalf of all children. We are far too small to get involved in national activities, but we do know what's going on! Fifty years ago on this day, thousands of innocent people lost their lives or got maimed by a nuclear bomb. Instead of learning a lesson from this tragedy, India has joined the bandwagon of nuclear countries which are, I do not know why, called 'an elite club'. All the money that is being wasted in making nuclear weapons and keeping our soldiers up in Siachen can be used to provide better living conditions to unfortunate people or to educate children who can go to a school intead of wiping cars at crossroads. Mr Prime Minister, what exactly are you trying to do? Is your objective to prove to the world that India is powerful because it has a nuclear bomb? You are simply making things worse with your dangerous mentality. I don't think bombs protect anybody. You don't get power by possessing arsenals. The whole situation is like as they say, 'a man wearing a turban but no clothes'. You are simply giving India a bad name, being so stubborn about the CTBT, as well as making things worse with Pakistan. You can surely do something about this and look into the wretched conditions that millions of your fellow countrymen live in.

NAVEENA (age 12)
Mayo College Girls' School, Ajmer

Preface

Every day when I tried to complete this book with a proper review of the latest evidence, I was interrupted by new discoveries. One of the most moving and instructive was the letter printed opposite; a proper reminder that all books on the subject should start with the name of the massacre at Hiroshima. My idea was to record faithfully what some of my old associates had contributed: visitors from Mars, Indian seers often acclaimed as the best in the business, comrades on the road to Aldermaston, poets who went off with the prizes – headed by Byron himself, not always so well known in his cataclysmic mood. But still the interruptions persisted, until here came the most inescapable:

> Yajshhiko Takeda was 13 years old on August 6, 1945. Yesterday he held up a picture he had painted of the huge fireball that descended that day from the sky, killing 140,000 people. He was four miles from ground zero, and survived unscathed by hiding under a bench. A sister, aged 16, died of burns two days after the blast; another sister died of cancer this year. Mr Takeda said Indians or Pakistanis would never have been so euphoric about last month's tests if they understood the slow poison of radioactivity.[1]

Indian summers have played a special part in my education, a whole series of them across a few decades, with even an Indian winter thrown in during this last period as a quite unexpected enlightenment. I went to Srinagar, chief city of Kashmir, on what turned out to be the coldest day of the year. Being a long-standing defender of India's claims about Kashmir, I felt I must not forgo another chance to see for myself. On the previous occasion some twenty years ago I had seen the rivers and the mountains in all their radiant beauty, and seen also why so many people treasured this as their homeland. Neither Jawaharlal Nehru's tryst with destiny nor Salman Rushdie's *Midnight's Children* would have been conceivable without Kashmir. Misinterpretation of the message from India is a peculiar perversion, since that message often comes in an especially fresh adaptation of the English language.

An Indian Summer was the title selected by James Cameron for the book which several of his friends came to believe was the most moving he had ever written.[2] It was naturally coloured by his love affair with Moni, a love which restored and renewed his life and, furthermore – most importantly for our present purposes – gave him a new perspective on India itself. Even with Moni at his side, he was not constantly looking inside himself; he had always scorned the idea that good reporters should turn autobiographers. To describe the world around him was the real challenge, and he never dodged it. He had previously reported the conduct of Indian political leaders more sympathetically and knowingly than any other witness of the scene. He had seen with his own eyes the infamies which British imperialism could leave in its tracks. None of the cool perpetrators of these crimes or follies in faraway London would receive any mercy from him. But he sometimes saw Indian leaders falter and fail too: not only Jawaharlal Nehru's successors, but Nehru himself. He could turn on his friends' heroes, even his lover's, with an equal ferocity. It is too painful to inscribe at this point the actual words in which James Cameron delivered that judgement on Nehru. It might almost be concluded that his purpose in writing *An Indian Summer* had been to face it without flinching. This is a matter of such consequence that we must explore it later.

Especially in India, Jimmy's combined wisdom and humanity was seldom absent for long. Better than anyone else, he could present his arguments in a world-wide perspective. It was he who had reported best on the insanities of the nuclear age, having been escorted by the American military authorities to witness the 1954 tests at Bikini. Then and thereafter, to his dying day, he was the reporter of the nuclear scene who did more than any other to tear aside the veil of lies which all governments engaged in the business drew across their actions. It was a curious misfortune for those who had arranged for a group of people to witness the spectacle of the Bikini mushroom cloud that James Cameron was included among them. He was supposed to be there to help frighten America's future enemies. Instead, he became the most potent advocate of nuclear disarmament as the only cure. And forty years after the Bikini explosions, the arguments about their method of spreading radioactive poison still persisted.

As we glance back at the nuclear arguments of the 1950s, it is only fair to record that two of the Prime Ministers actually in office were eager, if they could, to use their authority to bring this terrible invention under some form of international control. One was Nehru himself in New Delhi, who saw this as part of the essential role which his new independent India could play in world affairs. The other was Sir Winston Churchill in No. 10 Downing Street, who found himself involved, in this last campaign of his life, with some strange allies, such as Nehru, and some old enemies, among them the Tory party leadership and the mandarins of the Foreign Office.

Churchill's idea, and it was indeed a big one, was to stop the nuclear arms race before it started. So horrified was he in his final period in office about the potential damage of the manufacture of the H-bomb that he considered it necessary to make a supreme effort to secure negotiations with the leaders of the Soviet Union. When Stalin died in 1953, Churchill thought the time was right to seek negotiations with his successors, whoever they might be. Nothing need be lost, no bargaining hand forfeited, in such a process. He himself had usually favoured personal talks at the highest level as the way to settle the most important questions. Indeed, this may have been one aspect of the matter which made his potential partners in the United States or nearer home suspicious or at least wary; for he had in his time had some top-level negotiations with Soviet leaders in which allegedly he had been out-manoeuvred or persuaded to make concessions which later proved inadvisable. Churchill himself would bitterly contest such accusations; and, on any reckoning, here was an entirely novel situation which might involve the survival of the human race itself. The more he pondered the obstacles placed across his path, the more passionate he became in his desire to remove them. On the testimony of his own doctor, he became well-nigh obsessed on the subject;[3] but, amazingly, none of this was known to the outside world.

However, a debate which later became famous took place in the House of Commons on 1 and 2 March 1955. Churchill opened the proceedings – it was in fact his last major speech in the place – with a sombre account of the peril for the human race involved in the development of nuclear weapons, and how still greater exertions must be made by all concerned to find a remedy. He did not quite say in his opening speech how he himself had been thwarted in this endeavour. A little later, Aneurin Bevan spoke from the Labour benches; he thought he had detected a sudden reticence in Churchill's speech where he was bursting to say more. Could it be that Churchill wanted to meet the new Russian leaders but 'the United States leaders would not let him – a sombre thing to say, and a wicked thing to believe – that we have now reached the situation where Great Britain can, in a few short years, run the risk of the extinction of civilisation, and we cannot reach the potential enemy in an attempt to arrive at an accommodation with him because we are at the mercy of the United States?'[4] And then Churchill intervened, to speak more plainly than he had the day before. No, it was wrong, he said, to talk of United States dictation. It was true that he had wanted a top-level conference soon after Malenkov took power in Moscow, and had been ready to go to see President Eisenhower to persuade the Americans. But then – and this was the first hint the House had had of the matter – 'I was struck down by a very sudden illness which paralysed me completely.' Thereafter it had not been possible to persuade Eisenhower to 'join the process'. Somewhat later, as we shall see, the same or a slightly more enlightened Eisenhower did join the process; but there is no evidence that Churchill in 1955 was not wiser still. According to his doctor, at that particular moment of crisis, he accused both Eisenhower and his own Foreign Office of having 'bitched things up'.[5]

Jimmy Cameron's Indian summer was darkened by events in India itself and by the greater threat to the world at large. Just occasionally, and most monstrously as I felt, the two threats seemed to converge. If defence ministers in other continents argued that the only final defence against a nuclear threat was to have nuclear weapons themselves, how could the terrible logic not be applied elsewhere? And yet, when I first heard the proposition that there might be a nuclear arms race on the Indian sub-continent, I felt it was the ultimate insanity. I could not believe that intelligent Indian leaders would wish it to happen. Apart even from the direct perils involved with the weapons, such an imposition would mean the end of all hopes for a war against Indian poverty. How could it be that India – the politicians or the people – would be forced to that conclusion? For several years I went to India, seeking an answer and suspecting always that the threat to India was also a threat to the whole world. On this last such visit, in the autumn of 1997, I met a man whose passion on this theme reminded me of Jimmy Cameron. I had heard Indians speak their minds on this subject previously – among them Rajiv Gandhi, Indira Gandhi and Nehru himself – but this new recruit to the campaign for nuclear disarmament had a special right to be heard. He was Robert McNamara, formerly the Defense Secretary in the United States government. This book is prompted by his declarations. All the Indian leaders I have mentioned, and, of course, a host of others, would approve his proposal for world-wide nuclear disarmament.

*

I may perhaps be permitted to add here to the great reporter three other mentors, one of them especially also Jimmy's friend. Wherever either of them went on the business of nuclear disarmament, they would be in constant communi-cation. Little Vicky, the renowned cartoonist, invented the CND sign which went round the world. At least, I had always thought the design was Vicky's until the experts at CND's offices told me there were other claimants. Just the other day I saw a photograph of the 1998 German protest against those who were seeking to transport dangerous nuclear materials across their country. The huge crowd had formed itself into a CND sign.

The second mentor is H. G. Wells; no book about the bomb is complete without him. He wrote his special volume on the subject just after the first discoveries about the splitting of the atom and just before the outbreak of the 1914 war. The timing was perhaps one reason why proper attention was not paid to him then. The novel was entitled *The World Set Free*, since Wells hoped that the politicians would, if not at once, eventually understand what he was saying. The first extract reproduced here – written in 1914, I remind the reader again – recorded what he thought might be some of the first political reactions to his revelations, and the second how the trouble might spread to the continents most directly involved in this volume.

Certainly it seems now that nothing could have been more obvious to the people of the earlier twentieth century than the rapidity with which war was becoming impossible. And as certainly they did not see it. They did not see it until the atomic bombs burst in their fumbling hands. Yet the broad facts must have glared upon any intelligent mind. All through the nineteenth and twentieth centuries the amount of energy that men were able to command was continually increasing. Applied to warfare that meant that the power to inflict a blow, the power to destroy, was continually increasing. There was no increase whatever in the ability to escape. Every sort of passive defence, armour, fortifications and so forth, was being out mastered by this tremendous increase on the destructive side. Destruction was becoming so facile that any little body of malcontents could use it; it was revolutionising the problems of police and internal rule. Before the last war began it was a matter of

common knowledge that a man could carry about in a hand-
bag an amount of latent energy sufficient to wreck half a
city. These facts were before the minds of everybody; the
children in the streets knew them. And yet the world still,
as the Americans used to phrase it, 'fooled around' with the
paraphernalia and pretensions of war.[6]

A foretaste of the terrorists of the 1990s, as seen from 1914.
An amazing prophecy indeed; but he also foretold what
would happen if no collective international authority was
established.

> For the whole world was flaring then into a monstrous phase
> of destruction. Power after power about the armed globe
> sought to anticipate attack by aggression. They went to war
> in a delirium of panic, in order to use their bombs first.
> China and Japan had assailed Russia and destroyed Moscow,
> the United States had attacked Japan, India was in anarch-
> istic revolt with Delhi a pit of fire spouting death and flame;
> the redoubtable King of the Balkans was mobilising. It must
> have seemed plain at last to everyone in those days that the
> world was slipping headlong to anarchy. By the spring of
> 1959 from nearly two hundred centres, and every week
> added to their number, roared the unquenchable crimson
> conflagrations of the atomic bombs, the flimsy fabric of
> the world's credit had vanished, industry was completely
> disorganised and every city, every thickly populated area
> was starving or trembled on the verge of starvation. Most
> of the capital cities of the world were burning; millions of
> people had already perished, and over great areas govern-
> ment was at an end. Humanity has been compared by one
> contemporary writer to a sleeper who handles matches in
> his sleep and wakes to find himself in flames.[7]

However, the same H. G. Wells did also offer his remedy,
as up-to-date as the Indian fingers on the matches.

At times when the arguments about the bomb were especially vibrant or even vicious, the poets might put the case better than anyone else. What the 'nuclear winter' or the final act of extinction might involve became part of the argument itself. All those noted above had their say, and it might be supposed that not many could improve on the H. G. Wells of 1914. Yet there was one other who foresaw not only the scale of the destruction threatened but also the kind of dispute – chiefly religious – which would push the world over the edge into the catastrophe. In our nuclear campaigns, I used to ask the audience to guess the author. Once I heard Peggy Ashcroft, herself a passionate CNDer, recite this passage:

I had a dream, which was not all a dream.
The bright sun was extinguish'd, and the stars
Did wander darkling in the eternal space,
Rayless, and pathless, and the icy earth
Swung blind and blackening in the moonless air;
Morn came, and went – and came, and brought no day,
And men forgot their passions in the dread
Of this their desolation; and all hearts
Were chill'd into a selfish prayer for light:
And they did live by watch fires – and the thrones,
The palaces of crowned kings – the huts,
The habitations of all things which dwell,
Were burnt for beacons; cities were consumed,
And men were gathered round their blazing homes
To look once more into each other's face;
Happy were those who dwelt within the eye
Of the volcanoes, and their mountain-torch:
A fearful hope was all the world contain'd;
Forests were set on fire – but hour by hour
They fell and faded – and the crackling trunks
Extinguish'd with a crash – and all was black.

The brows of men by the despairing light
Wore an unearthly aspect, as by fits
The flashes fell upon them; some lay down
And hid their eyes and wept; and some did rest
Their chins upon their clenched hands, and smiled;
And others hurried to and fro, and fed
Their funeral piles with fuel, and looked up
With mad disquietude on the dull sky,
The pall of past world; and then again
With curses cast them down upon the dust,
And gnash'd their teeth and howl'd; the wild birds shriek'd,
And, terrified, did flutter on the ground,
And flap their useless wings; the wildest brutes
Came tame and tremulous; and vipers crawl'd
And twined themselves among the multitude,
Hissing, but stingless – they were slain for food:
And War, which for a moment was no more,
Did glut himself and; – a meal was bought
With blood, and each sate sullenly apart
Gorging himself in gloom; no love was left;
All earth was but one thought – and that was death,
Immediate and inglorious; and the pang
Of famine fed upon all entrails – men
Died, and their bones were tombless as their flesh;
The meagre by the meagre were devoured,
Even dogs assail'd their masters, all save one,
And he was faithful to a corpse, and kept
The birds and beasts and famish'd men at bay,
Till hunger clung them, or the dropping dead
Lured their lank jaws; himself sought out no food,
But with a pious and perpetual moan
And a quick desolate cry, licking the hand
Which answered not with a caress – he died.
The crowd was famish'd by degrees, but two
Of an enormous city did survive,
And they were enemies; they met beside

The dying embers of an altar-place
Where had been heap'd a mass of holy things
For an unholy usage; they raked up,
And shivering scraped with
Their cold skeleton hands
The feeble ashes, and their feeble breath
Blew for a little life, and made a flame
Which was a mockery, then they lifted up
Their eyes as it grew lighter, and beheld
Each other's aspects – saw, and shriek'd, and died –
Even of their mutual hideousness they died,
Unknowing who he was upon whose brow
Famine had written Fiend. The world was void,
The populous and the powerful – was a lump,
Seasonless, herbless, treeless, manless, lifeless –
A lump of death – a chaos of hard clay.
The rivers, lakes, and ocean all stood still,
And nothing stirred within their silent depths;
Ships sailorless lay rotting on the sea,
And their masts fell down piecemeal; as they dropp'd
They slept on the abyss without a surge –
The waves were dead; the tides were in their grave,
The moon their mistress had expired before;
The winds were withered in the stagnant air,
And the clouds perish'd; Darkness had no need
Of aid from them – She was the universe.[8]

Alongside Byron, the campaigners of the 1960s would also adapt Dylan Thomas:

> Do not go gentle into that good night, . . .
> Rage, rage against the dying of the light.

But none better than Adrian Mitchell, who exposed the lies about Vietnam and much else. Angela Carter saw him as a

Pied Piper, determinedly singing us away from catastrophe; but he also saw how

> the planet staggers like King Lear
> with his dead darling in his arms.

M.F.
November 1998

Chapter 1

New Voices from Asia

Choosing anti-nuclear Hiroshima as the site for an address to thirty thousand people in October 1957, Nehru expressed his hope that nuclear explosions would be stopped 'and that the terrible scourge and fear of warfare with atomic weapons will also be banned and ended'. May the key to Hiroshima, he said, 'prove a key to the heart of people all over the world, moving them to compassion, moving them to discard fear, and to live in friendship and cooperation with each other'.

Lawrence S. Wittner, *Resisting the Bomb*, vol. II

When India, the world's biggest democracy, staged its general election in the spring of 1998 – half a century after the Indians had wrested their independence from the British – its political leaders, of all shades of opinion, had plenty to argue about, not least the persistent, grinding poverty which seemed to hold an ever-increasing number of Indian families in its grip. The clash between rich and poor seemed to have grown sharper in modern times; several of the country's foremost leaders at the time of independence, headed by Mahatma Gandhi and Jawaharlal Nehru, and several of their closest friends in other countries, had prophesied that this would be the test for the future: how the new India, with the stultifying encumbrance of British imperialism off its back, would tackle the ancient and modern problem of Indian poverty. They have made some valiant efforts: the kind of famines which were tolerated under British rule as recently as the mid-1940s are at least recognized and curbed. But the requirement to deal with the real rich-and-poor problem is something almost out of a different world: we shall give an up-to-date hint of it later. Meanwhile, India has been wickedly distracted from pursuing its own interest by pressures from the supposedly wiser but certainly all-powerful Western world – headed by successive United States administrations, with the governments of Britain still acting as their obedient servants. The responsibility for what is happening – or what is *not* happening – in the attack on Indian poverty rests with us. Guilt is a better word.

I will set out a little later the sequence of events which has led to the tragedy. It involves a series of occasions when different choices were offered to Western leaders. For now, here are two brief reports published in *The Asian Age* of 26 and 27 February 1998, with the brief headlines devised by the paper itself which indicate some of the matters Indian voters were supposed to consider. Some aspects of both reports may be quite unfamiliar to English or American readers, but may I ask them to keep these passages to refer to when it is necessary to remind ourselves how Western arrogance may grate on Indian ears?

US worried by arms race in Pak, India

Washington: The US is concerned over 'strategic competition' between India and Pakistan in nuclear and missile potential, saying it is dangerous tarnishing the image of the two countries and causing concern among investors. 'US is concerned over the imperative, in some senses, of technology development, wherein the two states, without even intending to, could get into an arms race,' US State Department's regional affairs of South Asia bureau chief Robert K. Boggs said.

If voted in, BJP will make atom bomb

Hamirpur, Himachal, Pradesh: Senior Bharatiya Janata Party leader, Murli Manohar Joshi, said on Thursday, India would manufacture an atom bomb if his party was voted to power at the Centre.

Addressing election rallies here and in Sujanpur Tira in favour of the BJP candidate for Hamirpur Assembly seat, Ms Urmila Thakur, he alleged that successive Congress and United Front governments at the Centre had neglected the country's defence. As a result, the ISI of Pakistan had spread its network in India. Mr Joshi said there was great resentment among defence personnel over their service conditions and salaries.

Discussions about the bomb did play some part in the election. The Bharatiya Janata Party (BJP) sought to argue that its opponents in the previous administration had neglected the question. However, several of its predecessor governments had taken steps, much against their will but none the less deliberately, to enable India to make the bomb. At every stage when they did so, they made proposals to the West which could have avoided the whole development. On each occasion they had the door slammed in their faces. If previous administrations had not made these preparations, the attack of the BJP in this last election would have been even more bitterly xenophobic. But even these preparations involved what Washington's South Asia bureau chief, Robert K. Boggs, calls 'the imperative of technology development'. Since his country's relations with Pakistan had always been closer than with India, his knowledge of Pakistan's technological imperatives was precise and accurate. The nuclear race between India and Pakistan has already started and cannot easily be stopped. Who could properly be put in charge of such a development? It would need the combined genius of a new Stanley Kubrick and a new Peter Sellers to present 'Dr Strangelove, I presume'. It is the maddest scene in nuclear history, and it may be that we look in vain for an escape from Dr Strangelove's lunacy.

Throughout the whole period of Indian independence, from 1947 to the present day – with the exception only of the first few years after the original partition – a main feature of United States foreign policy has been to favour Pakistan against India. Over the same period British foreign policy has also been shaped to follow the American design. Both these propositions may be contested, but they are both true, as will be illustrated a little later. The British role has been especially pusillanimous; we should have been better able than the Americans to mark how perilous were developments in Pakistan and how important it was to help sustain democratic institutions in India. But all such considerations were cast aside to serve what was claimed to be the supreme strategic purpose. Nothing counted beside the military assessment, with the nuclear weapon available to be invoked in the last extremity. How often did military advisers from other countries listen to these debates and how soon might they too be forced to accept the inexorable logic? Only the nuclear weapon itself could provide the essential shield.

It was not, however, the Americans who were primarily responsible for the biggest display of ineptitude in pursuing their strategic objective and isolating India. It was the British who (with support and encouragement from President Eisenhower) went ahead with the plan which later became known as the Baghdad Pact. This was to be a defensive alliance of countries on the southern borders of the Soviet Union comparable with the North Atlantic

Treaty Organization devised for the self-defence of Europe. NATO had much to be said for it, and served its defensive purpose immediately and for several years thereafter. The so-called Baghdad Pact, signed in that city in the winter of 1955, had no such clear purpose or intelligent preparation. Instead of binding together the Arab states, which might have an eventual interest in resisting Soviet pressure, it tended to split them apart and expose the clashing interests of individual states in the area. As far as India was concerned the offence was especially sharp, but none of the Western leaders seem to have cared. The Baghdad Pact included Pakistan and excluded India. India could not have joined without abandoning the policy of neutrality between the so-called superpowers which it had pursued since independence. Everyone in the Western world knew that, but no one seemed to consider it important – except for Aneurin Bevan, whose lone voice protested vehemently in the House of Commons against the Labour party's support for the proposed alliance. In his view it was far more important to sustain a friendship with democratic India in the years ahead than to court all the other ramshackle states brought together under the pact. No benefit was derived from the pact by any signatory to it – except Pakistan, which henceforward became the recipient of British and American favours. Every Arab leader who had signed on the dotted line at Baghdad found himself labelled a British/American stooge, under increased threat to his life and his country as a consequence. By some ineffable process impossible to unravel, Baghdad had been selected by the brilliant Arab experts of the British Foreign Office as the honoured haven of Western authority in the resistance to communism. The Baghdad Pact was the last important fling of the old British Empire; within twelve months it was swept away by the abortive British attempt to seize the Suez Canal and destroy President Nasser in Cairo in the process.

During that eventful year of 1956, President Eisenhower entertained Prime Minister Nehru in Washington. They met just a few days after the Suez affair, and it might have been supposed that their shared outrage at that escapade would mark out for them a common interest in the future. Nehru condemned the British action as an imperialist crime, Eisenhower called it a monumental folly. This surely could have been the moment when the United States at the peak of its power recognized the different kind of greatness which India had achieved and the greatness, too, of the Indian leaders, with Nehru at their head. But Eisenhower's own record of the meeting showed how little he, like so many observers, understood the significance of the new India. He showed nothing but good manners towards Nehru himself. He was impressed, as everyone was, by the Indian leader's coolness, foresight and manner of expression. What he hopelessly under-rated was the role which the new India was to play in the world and which Nehru also sought to present with his customary clarity. India had chosen its policy of neutrality deliberately, not on any grounds of ideological preference. It was determined to guard the democratic freedoms which it had so recently gained. In the world at large, neutral powers were needed to keep the great powers apart. The doctrine happened to be very different from the one which Eisenhower's Secretary of State, John Foster Dulles, was seeking to impose; but the arguments for a different policy were firmly stated to the seemingly all-powerful President. No friend or ally could ever claim that India had not put the case fairly. India might fear attack from two countries, the Soviet Union and communist China, but they would only mount such an assault if India posed a threat to them or offered a tempting prize, and a neutral India fulfilled neither condition. 'Neutrality has another advantage,' Nehru continued: 'India and China have eighteen hundred miles of common border. Any attempt to maintain a defence of that long border would be such an expensive proposition as to render India completely unable to raise the standards of living of her people. Starvation and disease would make the nation even more susceptible to Communist penetration.'

Independent India was less than ten years old, but the condition of its people was such that the assault on their poverty must take precedence over everything else. A few years later, in 1962, China did make a military attack across that frontier. It was for Nehru the most damaging blow of his life, and yet the moral to be drawn from the wretched affair was not solely one of the need for military prepared-ness. It was still true that what India required was a con-certed, sustained attack on Indian poverty, and that a newly imposed military burden could destroy that hope altogether. If future Indian leaders, and maybe Nehru himself, drew the deduction that, however insufferable or exacting in economic terms, they must look to their defences, they could hardly be blamed.

President Eisenhower was an intelligent, sensitive man, and both his own country and the world at large were lucky to have him there when so much power, for good or evil, was increasingly being assembled in the United States itself and in the hands of its chief elected leader. Each American President, especially in the nuclear age, seemed to be a wiser man when he left office than when he arrived; this was certainly true in Eisenhower's case. His chief fault in the conduct of foreign policy was that he was too ready to follow the advice of his Secretary of State; and Dulles in turn was much too ready to believe that the modern world was divided into two blocs, the enemies of the United States and its friends. Any country which would not readily join the American-designed and American-directed anti-Soviet, anti-communist bloc must be considered an enemy. For India itself, as we have already noted, this was an impossible choice. But there was, throughout the 1950s, an argument of realpolitik which made the Dulles doctrine look like dangerous nonsense. Which side was China on? If there was any doubt, would not the Dulles doctrine keep it firmly fixed in alliance with the Soviet Union? Since 1945 several countries, including Britain and India, had argued that it would be much wiser to seek to secure for communist China its proper place on the United Nations Security Council. Nehru had in fact raised this question with Eisenhower privately when they met in 1956, and it was the one point on which Eisenhower gave him a dusty answer. In the President's eyes, Red China was as much of an enemy as the Soviet Union itself. The necessary clarification of the situation was still a few years away.

There was one other topic to which Nehru and Eisenhower would constantly return in their discussions, although they often found it even more intractable than communist China. 'Kashmir is a province,' Eisenhower was informed in his notes, 'the bulk of whose population is Muslim, like Pakistan's. It is controlled by India, a Hindu nation, and heated feelings remain from the bloody skirmishes between Indians and Pakistanis for control.'[1] How the original decision was made whereby Kashmir became part of India instead of Pakistan may be properly described as a combined moral, political and legal question. The legal aspect of it may be explained first. Whenever challenged on the matter, India's representative at United Nations meetings was able to supply the answer. For a period (1952–62) India's ambassador to the UN was V. K. Krishna Menon, and he could present the case with overwhelming relish and force. At the time of partition, since there was no democratic electorate to be consulted, the existing rulers in the different states made their choices between India and Pakistan. The man in charge in Kashmir was the Maharaja Hari Singh, himself a Hindu although the population of Kashmir was predominantly Muslim. After considerable hesitation he sided with India. However, the situation in the state, then and thereafter, was powerfully, maybe decisively, influenced by the activities of Sheikh Abdullah, the strongest Muslim leader in the area, who played a critical role in the commotions of the time and soon emerged as the first Prime Minister of the new state.

The association between Nehru and Abdullah, between Kashmir and India, should have been understood on its own. It was a key strand in the whole story of Indian independence. Abdullah was the leading Kashmiri supporter of the Indian struggle, but he had plenty of others at his side. No one had any excuse for misunderstanding. Several other features of the independence settlement with Britain Nehru and others of the Congress leaders hated, but if they had included a further provision that Kashmir would go with Pakistan his hand would have shrivelled rather than sign anything. Indeed, to do so would have been a betrayal of Abdullah too. At that time, the sympathy between them was perfect. Nehru's collection of essays published in London in 1941, significantly entitled *The Unity of India*, includes a chapter on Kashmir, the most powerful and moving in the book. Kashmir was Nehru's home no less than Abdullah's. 'Kashmir calls back, its pull is stronger than ever, it whispers its fairy magic to the ears, and its memories disturb the mind. How can they who have fallen under its spell release themselves from this enchantment?'[2] Once upon a time American Presidents read books as well as briefs and dispatches. Franklin Roosevelt had done so, and Theodore Roosevelt before him. Each for sure would have studied Nehru's writings. Our world cannot afford to neglect such treasures. No one should dare even to join the debate about Kashmir without studying the joint Nehru–Abdullah prologue to it.

Eisenhower, to do him credit, liked to see at first hand what was happening in the countries with which his own was allied, and in 1958 he went on an extended tour – not to Kashmir, where he could have heard the case from Abdullah himself, but to both the new Pakistan and the new India. In Karachi he was the honoured guest of President Ayub, who enlivened the proceedings with graceful requests for American aid: he spoke perfect English and displayed perfect manners, regretting only that some countries might choose to accept the aid without acknowledging America's generosity. He was deeply concerned about what the Russians might be doing across their northern border in Afghanistan; in earlier times, before the advent of the Soviet Union, it was across that territory the Russian Empire sought to expand. On his own domestic matters Ayub was hardly less candid. Soon after taking over, he said, it had been necessary to establish what Eisenhower called 'a virtual dictatorship'. Since several of the other countries the President visited on that same trip – Turkey, for example, and Afghanistan itself – were dictatorships with even more outward signs of authoritarian rule, Eisenhower was not deeply disturbed by the revelation. His own America was still recovering from the cataclysm of worldwide conflict and now seemed suddenly to be called upon to mobilize afresh against a new threat of world-wide communism. He could be pardoned if he saw the problem first through the eyes of his own country before considering the plight of others.

The US President had the grace to acknowledge that what he saw next, on crossing into India, was something quite beyond his expectation or experience. Some special laurels were hung round his neck, even before the Indians greeted him with their traditional favours. He was the leader of the great republic which had fought and won the victory over fascism. He was the leader of the nation which had condemned the British infamy in Suez. He was the true friend of their leader, or so they believed, and they assembled in their tens of thousands to hear what each would say. Not only had Eisenhower himself never seen such a spectacle, Nehru himself was inspired by it to see a fresh hope for his people and his country. Indian democracy mobilized in such a manner had been responsible for the expulsion of the British. Now it could be mobilized for even larger, long-lasting purposes. Crowds had come in their scores of thousands to join the assembly in Connaught Circle, New Delhi, to hear the President of the United States. It was a special kind of Indian salute to the part which liberal America had played in India's liberation and India's hopes for the future. It was the clearest possible expression of the view which Nehru himself wished to present to his influential visitor: that the policy of non-alignment was not some sinister plot against Eisenhower's Secretary of State and his country but a powerful aid in mapping out different and wiser courses for humankind generally. If some further military force was what India was being called upon to offer, it could do little. But if what was wanted was an intelligent, persistent pursuit of other possibilities, India – especially with a democratically elected ruler like Nehru in charge – could play an indispensable part.

Sometimes the horrific, incalculable power which the invention of nuclear weapons placed in the hands of political leaders made them look like monsters; but sometimes, too, they would scrutinize carefully what their own scientists told them, and they would return to their senses. In the late 1940s and 1950s, when the testing of the weapons was still in a comparatively primitive stage, nothing like a guarantee existed that these gleams of sanity on either side of the Iron Curtain could be synchronized. On the contrary: outbreaks of hysteria on one side could feed outbreaks on the other. The United States government always claimed that it exercised a much firmer, or at least more open, political control over the military than the Soviet Union. But there were some horrifying lapses. When the American armies were in North Korea in the early 1950s, the rumour was that General MacArthur wished to threaten the use of the atomic bomb and that the visit by British Prime Minister Clement Attlee to President Truman in Washington helped to stop it. A more palpable example was what happened in the 1949 dispute with Red China over the offshore islands of Matsu and Quemoy. Again it looked as if the Americans, having intervened with a major military force, were suffering a serious defeat. They did contemplate using what they called 'small-yield' atomic weapons against hostile airfields on the Chinese mainland but, having no international backing, held back. The British Foreign Secretary at the time, Selwyn Lloyd, learned of the matter only on reading Eisenhower's memoirs. To have used the new weapons in either of these situations would indeed have been an outrage; but President Eisenhower was eager to learn.

During his presidency Eisenhower assembled the biggest war machine ever constructed. Nothing like it had ever been seen before, not even in wartime itself: nothing developed with such speed; nothing able to call so readily for a response from the scientific laboratories where the latest discoveries were being made, especially in the field of nuclear weapons; nothing so monstrous in the diversion of materials and money from peace-making to war-making purposes. It was this machine which henceforth protected the peace of the whole planet, for the benefit not merely of the Americans themselves but of everyone else who was clever enough to take shelter with them. This is still the nature of American nuclear supremacy. It must be honestly faced, with all its implications for other individual countries, and we shall do so a little later.

Here and now, however, we must examine further Eisenhower's motives and actions at this period. He took some pride in the war machine which he was creating, but he never departed from the doctrine that it was a second-best choice imposed upon him by the combined power, intransigence and trickery of the rulers of the communist world. He followed with skill and care all the elaborate, detailed discussions with the Soviet representatives to see whether there could be a safe road towards disarmament instead of rearmament. He was never persuaded of the Soviet Union's good faith in such negotiations, although he believed that its overwhelming interest could eventually push it in that direction.

He would often return to this charge of perfidy against the Soviet leaders in their negotiations, as if this were the main cause – indeed, the sole cause – of the eventual breakdown of diplomatic efforts to find a solution. Sometimes this truly was the reason, this combined with the forms of espionage in which the Soviet leaders engaged and the sudden exposure of activities which could destroy public confidence in any treaty obligations previously agreed. However, the most notorious of all these disruptions was the one which wrecked the proposed disarmament discussions scheduled for Paris in May 1958. For about two years the United States air force, with Eisenhower's approval, had been conducting espionage flights across Soviet territory, chiefly for the purpose, as the Americans claimed, to take precautions against developments on the Soviet side which could assist surprise attacks. However, the American flights were a new and more sophisticated form of espionage – no one could deny that, and if proof were needed, even the British government at the time, despite its friendship with the United States, at first refused permission for such flights to take off from British soil.

The main obstacle from the Soviet side to a conclusive negotiation often seemed to be their absolute rejection of any serious inspection system to ensure that commitments made at conferences were fulfilled in the domestic factories and laboratories. The need for such a system was clear enough: without provisions for detailed inspection, disarmament conventions could be worthless. Unhappily, in Eisenhower's period, there was no time to explore the paradox that the further development of nuclear arsenals also enhanced the incapacity to hide them. We shall of course return to this all-important aspect of the matter later.

During his own presidency and later, Eisenhower followed all these developments with the utmost care. He was especially encouraged in his last months in office when he studied the capacity of the Polaris submarine for carrying the nuclear warhead. Such instruments could not be the victims of the kind of surprise attack which figured in all

the disarmament discussions. The United States was excruciatingly sensitive on this subject, since the Second World
War had started for them with a surprise assault which the
aggressors believed could settle the outcome there and then.
Neither he nor anyone else was entitled to take a fresh risk
in such matters. But again we may note the longer and
wiser perspective from which he never wished to escape.
For him, the war machine which he had created was no final
protection. That must still be sought at the disarmament
negotiating table, however distant or complex the prospect
might seem to be. It would benefit some later American
leaders to study the kind of wisdom which Eisenhower
sought to instil. And lest any of them complain that he did
not speak plainly enough, we may quote the actual speech:

> This conjunction of an immense military establishment and
> a large arms industry is new in the American experience.
> The total influence – economic, political, even spiritual –
> is felt in every city, every state house, every office of the
> federal government. We recognise the imperative need for
> this development. Yet we must not fail to comprehend its
> grave implications. Our toil, resources, and livelihood are
> all involved; so is the very structure of our society. In the
> councils of government, we must guard against the acquisi-
> tion of unwarranted influence, whether sought or unsought,
> by the military industrial complex. The potential for the
> disastrous rise of misplaced power exists and will persist.[3]

Perhaps that account of his own stewardship and the moral
to be drawn from it was the most important service Eisenhower performed for his people. These were not the words
of a power maniac; indeed, he thought such power might
go to the heads of rulers, elected or non-elected. If it was
conceivably workable, such deadly machines must be democratically controlled.

Within a few years the whole apparatus was put to an extraordinary test. In one sense, the Cuban crisis could be seen as America's Kashmir. Americans did not like the idea of outsiders thinking they had the right to interfere in their hemisphere any more than Indians liked Americans laying down the law to them about Kashmir. If this seemed to be a case of excessive hemispherical sensitivity, it was one of America's great Presidents who established their case. Whatever else it was or was not, the Cuban crisis was a grave offence against the Monroe Doctrine.

If Eisenhower himself could give an impression of a cool military appreciation of the nuclear peril, some of his fellow chiefs in the United States high command could reveal, in the hours of crisis and decision, a quite different temperament. The most famous of all these confabulations took place in the White House over fourteen days in 1962, in what was called the Cuban Missile Crisis. Thanks to one innovation introduced by President Kennedy soon after he had succeeded Eisenhower, the installation of tape recorders in the Oval Office, a far more extensive record of what was actually said in the discussions which led to the effective American decision than would formerly have been available is there for all to read. Each of the participants in these conversations has sought to give his own account of what he said. But the so-called Kennedy tapes have a special authenticity; maybe Kennedy himself would not have chosen this method of reporting, if he had known how the records would read thirty or forty years later. At roughly the same time as these tapes were made public in 1997,[4] a quite unexpected Russian contribution to the history of the crisis was discovered. Two skilled Russian Academicians – having been able to investigate previously secret archives in the Kremlin – have offered a comprehensive

account of the Cuban crisis from 1958 to 1964; an examination not only of the Soviet Union's policy but also of the
conduct of the individual communist leaders. And a further
boon offered at the time of publication of both these extraordinary works was an extensive review of them in *The
Times Literary Supplement* of 6 February 1998 by Edward
N. Luttwak, Senior Fellow at the Center for Strategic and
International Studies, Washington DC, an institution not
normally associated in the public mind with radical ideas
of nuclear disarmament. The Luttwak judgement on the
whole affair is one of persistent significance. He – or the
TLS editor – called his essay: 'The great turning: how
the Cuban crisis shaped the rest of the cold war'. A strange
exaggeration, I would claim, but a pardonable one. The
title of the book by the Russian Academicians was '*One Hell
of a Gamble*': a truer representation, maybe. It was the precise moment when our planet came nearest to nuclear
annihilation. We are entitled to pause and give some credit
to the endeavours of all the authors listed above.

The origin of this particular crisis was the readiness of
Nikita Khrushchev, the Soviet leader, to carry his support
of Fidel Castro and his recently established regime in Cuba
forward to the point of establishing on his territory a range
of nuclear weapons which, if ever used, could inflict appalling damage on the United States itself. One excuse for his
action was that Cuba was an independent state whose newly
established regime the Americans had sought to destroy by
a military invasion. It could be claimed that the purpose of
the nuclear installations was defensive: to ward off another
attack. Moreover, if the proximity of nuclear bases to the
American mainland was the real problem, the offence was
not all on one side: the Americans had recently established
nuclear bases not so far from the Soviet Union, most

notably in Italy and Turkey. Especially in the latter case, Khrushchev could claim that the stationing of Jupiter missiles in Turkey was a perpetual offence, at least as menacing to his country as any threat from Cuba to the United States. Some of these factors may seem quite extraneous to the scandalous Soviet threat to the United States; but all of them figured in the disputations between Khrushchev and Kennedy, and all played some part in the final settlement.

Edward Luttwak's judgements on these and other kindred matters in the dispute, as expressed in his *TLS* essay, cannot be accepted as final, but nor can they be dismissed as the ravings of an obsessive nuclear disarmer. In particular, his verdict on the contrasted performances of the two chief actors on that stage, Kennedy and Khrushchev, cannot be dismissed as a fantasy. In his assessment – not stated in this precise language, but none the less inescapable – the world owed its survival of the Cuban crisis more to Khrushchev's eventual timidity, despite all his brazen displays over its course, than to Kennedy's persistent bravado. Several of Khrushchev's most enthusiastic supporters in the Soviet Union itself, and indeed Fidel Castro in Cuba, thought he had been forced into a humiliating surrender; some of his associates or rivals in the Kremlin drew the same conclusion and used it as part of their pretext for driving him out of office two years later. But from any point of view, and especially that of the people in the Soviet Union, this was a mistaken conclusion. If ever the so-called nuclear deterrent was intelligently deployed, it was by Khrushchev in the Cuban Missile Crisis. He had forced some American concessions nearer home; he had saved Castro; and he had then stepped back from the nuclear precipice.

According to Luttwak, no such favourable verdict could

be passed on the conduct of President Kennedy. He kept his nerve to the end; and, since Khrushchev eventually conceded, poker players must be inclined to applaud his achievement. But this was not a poker game; it was the moment when the leading political and military experts were most closely confronted with what the consequences of nuclear war would be, not only for their enemies but for their own people too. Fortunately for us all, Khrushchev was well informed on this subject – which is why he drew back. But, incredible as it may seem in a matter of such significance, Kennedy did not have at his disposal such accurate and disinterested advice as was available to Khrushchev – not on the matter of the destructiveness of nuclear weapons but on the intricate diplomatic-cum-intelligence questions about the way the Soviet leader shaped his decisions. Despite the supposed proficiency and huge cost of the United States intelligence services, Kennedy received from them, and more especially from his brother Robert, a stack of information which eventually proved worthless. He naturally listened with the utmost care to all his informants and, if he weighed their advice by their rank and experience, only one conclusion was possible. He must stand firm, whatever the consequences.

According to the tapes, only two voices were raised in opposition. One was that of the Commandant of the Marine Corps, General David Shoup, the least eminent of the military chiefs, who stuttered out his objection that they were misreading the significance of Khrushchev's Cuban adventure. If the Russians were going to bomb America they could do it from elsewhere. Kennedy seemed momentarily impressed; but then Curtis LeMay, founder and long-standing head of the Strategic Air Command, answered his junior's objection: 'We made pretty strong statements about the nuclear Cuba, that we would take action against offensive weapons. I think that a blockade, and political talk, would be considered by a lot of our friends and neutrals as being a pretty weak response to this. And I'm sure a lot of our citizens would feel that way too. You're in a pretty bad fix, Mr President.'[5]

With the sole exception of Commandant Shoup all the President's military advisers, including the joint chiefs under General Maxwell Taylor, continued throughout the whole crisis to advocate aerial bombardment, with an eventual actual invasion. It was this last addition to the list of recommended actions which upset the whole proposition. Invasions could be costly in human lives and maybe ineffective, as the American experience the year before in the Bay of Pigs had proved. But what could the aerial bombardments achieve? They could not capture the newly installed nuclear bases, and they could not be sure to destroy them. Yet throughout the whole argument the military chiefs continued to advocate their hopeless solution. Kennedy was bound to listen to them, but fortunately he was not persuaded. He knew the fix he was in; he knew better even than General LeMay how his fellow American citizens would construe any signs of weakness. However, he had some advisers in his midst prepared to advocate caution – for which there were plentiful reasons, as Khrushchev's eventual withdrawal proved. The most important voice raised in opposition to the military chiefs was that of the civilian head of the defence ministry, Robert McNamara. Like his President, he had only been in office a short period, and again like him, he had little direct military experience of his own; but he had the courage and intelligence to say 'No' to his supposed superiors. He was absolutely opposed to the use of force in those circumstances. He was for some critical hours the wisest voice in the Western world, and one always worth listening to thereafter.

Occasionally, despite these hours of crisis, or maybe because of them, the world's leaders edged back from the precipice; but considering the risks involved, this was a painfully slow process and even the first shaky footholds with which they seemed content looked wretchedly insecure. This was also the first great age of the anti-nuclear campaigners, the Aldermaston marchers. We shall trace their contribution more closely in the next chapter.

I append here the extraordinary last paragraph which Mr Luttwak wrote in his February 1998 comment on the 1962 Cuban crisis. It may come in useful later, since it is the clearest proof that American Secretaries of Defense and even American Presidents were occasionally struck by the simple wisdom of the Aldermaston marchers. If readers think this too tall a claim, they might postpone reading it until they have come to the end of this chapter.

> As for the American policy elite, the eventual consequence of the Crisis was to persuade much of it, with McNamara in the lead, that nuclear weapons were to be built at times and negotiated away at times, but never, ever to be used – though it was not until Ronald Reagan came to power that the US acquired a President, far removed from elite thinking as he was, who calmly told his shocked and disbelieving military chiefs that he would never authorise any use of nuclear weapons, contrary to NATO pledges and the assumptions built into all their major military plans.

As for Britain's view of the Cuban crisis, Prime Minister Harold Macmillan pronounced it a reckless gamble on the part of the Soviet leaders and Khrushchev himself which had been brilliantly and peacefully parried by President

Kennedy. Macmillan had indeed been kept in touch with Kennedy throughout the whole affair, but his account of it in his memoirs bears little relation to Luttwak's report cited above.[6] Macmillan knew nothing of the false intelligence reports with which Kennedy was fed; nothing of the superior advice available to Khrushchev; and not much of the huge pressure which the military advisers were exerting and which Kennedy, with the help of Robert McNamara and a few others, managed to resist. The stance Kennedy took did force Khrushchev to retreat without using the weapons; but the risks he also took can still make reporters or historians tremble. The most intelligent verdict to be passed on the whole affair was that it emphasized the necessity for all the parties concerned to return to the negotiating table where the larger questions of the nuclear threat could be examined and brought under some form of international control. Some of those involved did indeed draw this conclusion, and the path was thus opened for fresh negotiations on a comprehensive ban on nuclear tests which took place in Moscow. The interval between the crisis in October 1962 and the settlement of the Test Ban Treaty (TBT) in February 1963 was indeed comparatively short – an indication, perhaps, of how properly scared the world's leaders had become.

Jawaharlal Nehru watched these events with a growing but poignant interest. He wanted to see his India playing a leading role among the peace-makers on the international scene. Already in the 1950s his India spoke with a new voice at the meetings of the UN General Assembly. The voice happened to be that of V. K. Krishna Menon. Some people considered that he talked too stridently in criticism of the great powers, but most intelligent observers could see also that this new voice of a new country had a special right to be heard. India had not been present at the San Francisco conference of 1945 when the United Nations had been founded; now it was making up for lost time. The doctrine it preached, whether stridently or not, was the necessary one: if the world was being divided into two blocs, neither of which possessed the ultimate wisdom, then a third voice must be heard. India spoke for itself, but for many others too.

And yet, in 1962 Nehru had to turn aside from all such aspirations to face an entirely different crisis, one that lay quite outside his previous experience and seemed to shatter all his other hopes. His crisis, India's new crisis, came to a head during the most hectic days of the Cuban stand-off. No doubt that was part of the reason why the Chinese leaders chose that precise moment to attack; timing apart, the assault was one of the most monstrous crimes in history. The attack was launched across that undefended frontier which Nehru had discussed with Eisenhower a few years earlier. It was still undefended. Nehru and his defence minister, Krishna Menon, were naturally held responsible for allowing such a grievous exposure to persist, however unpardonable the Chinese treachery might be. Immediate offers of military help came from America and Britain. How could the aggression be stopped? How could it ever have been allowed to happen?

If the violence of the Chinese aggression was exacerbated by its suddenness, it was also the case that Nehru had seen the approach of the darkening cloud and had had to prepare his country for a profound change in its defence policies. He would have to accept the military burden which he feared would crush so many of his other hopes for his people. He hated what he had to do, and it would not be surprising if some of his responses to this unwelcome challenge seemed inconsistent or hesitant. His own military advisers and several of his political friends had long urged him to take action to deal with a quite different problem in the Indian territory of Goa, where the Portuguese Empire still exercised authority and was showing no readiness to remove itself as the British had done in 1947. In December 1961 Nehru agreed that the Indian army should take the necessary steps to occupy Goa. No doubt part of the reason was to inform others, above all the Chinese, that India did indeed have an army. The occupation proceeded peacefully, but some observers called it naked aggression. A UN Security Council resolution calling for a ceasefire was vetoed by the Soviet Union; two days later, a ceasefire by the Chinese forces in the north was ordered by the Chinese leaders, as suddenly as they had launched the original attack. The Soviet intervention was the most interesting aspect of the affair. If China was to become obstreperous, no one could be surprised if India turned elsewhere for aid. Throughout many months in 1962 discussions proceeded between the Indians and the Russians about the supply of fighter aircraft, a fleet of MiGs for India's defence programme. When the British and American defence departments discovered this developing relationship they expressed concern that Nehru himself was seeking to keep the matter secret. On the contrary, it is arguable that from India's point of view the more a potentially aggressive China knew of India's growing friendship with the Soviet Union the better.

What the Chinese incursion had done most precisely was to develop a strategic route for the supply of aid to Pakistan, to help show who might be master of that other Kashmir frontier. In days to come – years to come – that might appear to be the most serious outcome of the Chinese aggression. Pakistan had an ally which would stick with it through thick and thin, not caring in the least what infamies the Pakistan leaders might inflict on their own people.

Both the British and the American experts – the politicians and their advisers alike – misread the situation after the Chinese war: 'misreading' indeed is a mild term for the grave errors of judgement which vastly contributed to the burdens India had to carry in the future. On the question of Kashmir, both the British and the American leaders would protest that they were holding the balance between Pakistan and India, although it is hard to credit that they believed their own self-deception. Kashmir was already a part of India; to initiate the discussion on any other footing was to accept Pakistan's case. To imagine that India could easily be weaned away from this conclusion was an absurdity – especially, it might be said, while Prime Minister Nehru was still alive. Those who came after him were no less aware of the overwhelming evidence of the facts of the case and the most obvious repercussions. To seek to wrench Kashmir out of the Indian state would threaten the rest of the union; large numbers of Muslims and other minorities would be encouraged to believe that independent India offered no protection for them. To advance such a proposition at any time was dangerous enough; it was particularly offensive to make it when India was still smarting from defeat at the hands of China and when a so-called independent Kashmir might be happily received as a convenient piece of booty to reward their aggression. In London, Macmillan congratulated himself that he had somehow 'forced' Nehru and the Pakistani premier to meet. Mostly the Americans followed the British example, although the overriding interest for them, as for Britain, was this military choice. Henceforth, Pakistan's leaders knew that they had firm supporters in the West, whatever misdemeanours they committed at home, whereas democratic India would have to look elsewhere for its protection. It had already discovered some new friends in the Soviet Union and it would have been strange indeed if it had not sought to cultivate them. One highly qualified observer who marked these developments at close quarters was the American ambassador in New Delhi, J. K. Galbraith. He was deeply saddened by the combined blindness and presumption of his own country's attitude to India at that critical moment. He thought that much more could have been achieved by a better understanding of India's case, starting with Kashmir.

Jawaharlal Nehru's last months in office, indeed his last two years, were darkened by the awareness of India's military weakness. It was this single sin, if sin it was, which threatened to destroy the rest of his achievements as the foremost architect of Indian freedom and independence. This weakness was reflected not only in the consequences of the brutal Chinese aggression and his particular misjudged reaction to it – he talked from Delhi as if the people of Assam had already been overrun when they were still resisting – but also in the assessments which interested observers were prompted to make of the comparative virtues and strengths of Pakistan and India. Even in Eisenhower's time Pakistan, as we have seen, could stage impressive military parades; later, the lapses into military rule were yet more apparent. Some of these observers were applying some of these comparisons to Nehru's beloved Kashmir. The Chinese thought that they might soon collect some advantages for their allies there; but India's protection of the Kashmir frontier was more effective than might have been expected. Nehru committed the further error – or crime – of placing his old friend Sheikh Abdullah in protective custody lest he be tempted to favour Pakistan: a proof indeed, as it turned out, of how deeply each cared about Kashmir. Nehru could not conceive of an India without Kashmir; and the Sheikh, to his honour, despite all provocations, accepted the same conclusion.

Indira Gandhi, Nehru's loving and beloved daughter, watched these excruciating scenes with special fascination. She was her father's closest friend, but she was not yet seen as a possible successor to him as Prime Minister. The only political post which she had been prepared to occupy, chiefly on his prompting, was that of President of the Congress Party, a role she had filled reasonably well since 1959. She had witnessed at first hand how political direction at the centre could shape the hopes and fears of the Indian people. She went to Assam at the time of the Chinese attack and felt the lash meant for her father across her own back. She went to the Kashmir frontier and saw Indian soldiers needing nothing but decent direction to be able to resist and win. She went to a United Nations meeting in New York and had her first taste of unthinking American patronage of her father and her country. She could see for herself how India's enemies could exploit its weaknesses, and maybe made up her mind to seek other remedies. When her father died on 28 May 1964 she had equipped herself for the task of succession; but she took nothing for granted. The man backed by the other Congress leaders to take over from her father – Lal Bahadur Shastri – did approach her to ask if she would take the job, but she refused. She wanted to supervise the commemorations for her father and, as Congress leader, she soon found herself with plenty of other political commitments. Not exactly by design, but none the less by a fortunate coincidence she found herself in Srinagar in August 1965 when Pakistan's forces once more invaded the Kashmir valley. She stayed on to give moral support to the Indian forces resisting the aggression, and her presence was appreciated by soldiers and civilians alike. She insisted on being taken by helicopter to the Hajipir Pass where the fighting was fiercest, and returned to Delhi to tell Prime Minister Shastri that she knew more about the war than he did. Intervention from outside was needed to stop the fighting, and a summit meeting was held in Tashkent, where the Soviet leaders acted as mediators between Prime Minister Shastri and President Khan. Indira Gandhi was learning all the time and she would prefer that such meetings should take place under Indian auspices. Shastri signed the Tashkent Agreement on the morning of 10 January 1966; that night he died of a heart attack. One of the treaty's provisions restored the disputed pass to Pakistan, and if he had not died he would have had to face a political crisis. This was the point at which Indira's succession to her father's position was confirmed. It was not the happiest moment to succeed, but at least she had the compensation that henceforth she would deal directly with this question, one of such significance for the whole future of India and its relations with Pakistan. Tashkent was a compromise, reached partly by international pressure, but its adjustment of frontiers involved no Indian abandonment of principle. The next negotiations on these points, questions critical for the whole future of the sub-continent, would take place when Indira Gandhi was at the peak of her authority and when she exerted it with a combined skill and magnanimity which Nehru himself could not have surpassed. She could not achieve such results on her own; she would never make such foolish egotistical claims. But she understood the strengths and weaknesses of India and of the Congress Party of which she was now the elected leader. She applied her mind and her new political power to the task of building up India's real strength and its self-esteem. She performed this role so well that when the next election came in India – in 1969 – she secured an overwhelming victory.

In the matter of relations with its neighbour, India's successes were largely shaped by Pakistan's failures. But that had always been part of India's case. After independence, India had deliberately set out on the democratic road; Pakistan had no such aim or capacity. West Pakistan and East Pakistan were even more monstrously divided in the original partition than India itself, and when West Pakistan used its customary state power to keep control over its people, those people looked more and more to India for comfort and protection. They were Muslims, but many of their leaders, as in Kashmir, had played their part in the independence struggle. They thought they must fight for it afresh and they had brave leaders ready to do it. Freedom-loving people in India, along with their Prime Minister, naturally looked on these developments with an ever-increasing fascination. Defeats for Pakistan were victories for India, but here was evidence of what the best leaders of India had always proclaimed: India could offer better safety and protection for Muslims than Pakistan itself. A real chance appeared to heal the wound of partition inflicted on the country in 1947 and every effort must be made to profit from it.

At first, however, the blessing certainly looked a mixed one; when the military authorities in West Pakistan sought to address the situation by ruthlessly suppressing the revolution in East Pakistan, one terrible consequence was that hordes of refugees poured over the frontier into India itself. In the face of such a measureless human calamity, it looked at first as if Indira and her fellow Indian ministers had no remedy; no satisfactory military response either to the forces Pakistan had unleashed in the east or to the consequent pressure on India's own frontiers. Some of the responses she made may have looked weak, but they had their purpose. She went to America to seek aid in assisting the mass of refugees; she emerged from a meeting with President Nixon not exactly with nothing, but with nothing adequate to meet the crisis. He and his country had problems of their own in that part of the world, and whatever else she did, Indira Gandhi could not bolster the hopeless American case in Vietnam. She returned to New Delhi to face some desperate military choices of her own. If India did not use its military strength, the popular outrage of the Indian people might be overwhelming. If she gave the order for action, other hazards must be accepted: how swift could the Indian mobilization be, and how swift might be the reaction of the Chinese, who had retaliated in similar circumstances before – or even of the Americans, who had a powerful fleet not so far away and had already shown themselves more interested in friendship with Pakistan than with India? A series of excruciatingly difficult choices had to be made. To guide her in these she had, as she was always eager to acknowledge, an Indian commander-in-chief, S. H. J. Manekshaw, who would offer his advice without flinching. If there had been mistiming or misapplication of resources, the catastrophe could have been immeasurable. If Indira had acted earlier, she would not have had the military means to achieve decisive victory; if she had waited longer, the Chinese/American counter-strike might have pre-empted her new gains. At the moment of initial success, several voices urged a final military counter-attack on West Pakistan itself. She asked what the further casualties might be, and held her hand. The prize she wanted was a settlement with Pakistan which would endure, and she thought it was now within her grasp.

Mrs Gandhi chose Simla as the place where intelligent, long-lasting settlements might be sought: an end to the Pakistan–India quarrel over Kashmir, but also agreements on other matters. The stunning defeat inflicted on Pakistan's military leaders, who had plunged their country into such dangerous courses, meant their immediate removal from the scene, and a civilian leadership had been restored in the person of President Zulfikar Ali Bhutto.

At that particular moment Bhutto appeared as representative of a defeated, near-demoralized party to the dispute; but he had a style and vitality of his own and he wanted to play a leading role in his country's future. Indira wanted that too, in India's interest no less than Pakistan's. She did what she could to establish his status and authority, and thereby to ensure that the agreements they reached would be accepted as genuine and definitive. She went to Simla on her own the day before they were to meet, to ensure that everything was decently prepared for President Bhutto and his daughter Benazir. India had won the war, and with a spectacular speed which few observers expected; but Indira wanted no triumphalism. What she did want, if she could get it, was an acceptance of a future in which Pakistan and India could set aside their quarrels. A series of fresh disputes had been provoked by the war itself, but most of these were soluble, given intelligent goodwill on both sides. Much the most intractable was Kashmir; neither leader could return to his or her home territory and declare a surrender. According to the formula agreed at Simla, neither was required to do so. But India had secured the long-lasting assurance which it needed: each side abjured the resort to force, and all issues between the two countries were henceforth to be resolved bilaterally. That was the basis on which India took its stand for the future. It was an intelligent and honourable stance, superseding all the ambiguities of the past and seeking to mark out a much more adventurous future for the whole sub-continent. When Mrs Gandhi defended the agreement in the Indian parliament a few days later and was assailed for some concessions she had made to the defeated, she raised the whole tone of the argument: 'The time has come when Asia must wake up to its destiny, must wake up to the real needs of its people, must stop fighting amongst ourselves, no matter what our previous quarrels, no matter what the previous hatred and bitterness. The time has come today when we must bury the past.'[7]

The aftermath of Simla should have been a moment when India and Pakistan – or, better still, Indira Gandhi's Asia – abjured the further monstrous absurdity of a nuclear arms race all of their own. If there had been an intelligent international authority in operation covering these matters, each country might have turned to it for guidance and protection. But, as we shall see in a moment, the authority which did exist had a serious deficiency, and meanwhile the governments in both countries felt that they could not neglect the possibility of securing for themselves the capacity to develop nuclear weapons. Which country did it first later became a matter of contention. In fact, both made secret preparations at roughly the same time. The economic consequences of the lesser arms race which had resulted in the Pakistan aggression were already cruel enough. Once more, as after the Chinese aggression, the attack on India had been postponed. Every Indian leader since independence knew how much could be achieved to alleviate the country's pressing domestic problems with even the limited available resources. Now, these precious resources were diverted on a massive scale into the insatiable military machines. Pakistan accepted this wretched choice more readily than India. Irrespective of the occasional interventions from Bhutto, it was increasingly transformed into a military state, ruled by soldiers; and Pakistan's backers, headed by the Americans and the Chinese, would just as soon deal with military men as with obstreperous democratic politicians. Even after Pakistan's shameful aggression against India, even after its subsequent humiliations, the Americans still seemed to prefer Pakistan as an ally; and after the brief Bhutto interval they soon found an amenable and softly spoken general to take over.

To do them justice, the so-called great powers in the nuclear field had recognized the peril looming and had taken the first steps to try to ensure that it was contained. Their instrument – the Non-Proliferation Treaty (NPT), signed in 1970 – was imperfect, but had a truly serious purpose. Along with the Test Ban Treaty, signed in 1963, it represented the most successful effort hitherto to impose international controls upon the nuclear arms race. It sought to ensure that those who possessed the means to make nuclear weapons would not allow this capacity to be distributed to others. It did not include more effective means than were contained in the TBT for stopping the tests and their manufacture. It did contain a pious preamble suggesting that the existing nuclear powers must look to the time when full abolition could be considered.

Despite its good intentions this proposition had, from India's viewpoint and indeed from that of several other countries, some serious deficiencies. It seemed to divide the nations into those who were fit to have access to nuclear power and those who were not, and to assume that once this dividing line had been made it could never be crossed.

India, specifically, would have to accept that China permanently possessed nuclear power and India was denied it. After the Chinese aggression of 1962, no responsible Indian leader could accept such a doctrine. It would be a new form of apartheid; and it would never work. India argued instead for a much more genuine international settlement which modern science was making as feasible as the weapons themselves; full-scale disarmament with effective protection.

On 18 May 1974, it was announced that the Indian scientists had successfully detonated a nuclear device in Pokhran. It was, said one observer, 'the best-kept Indian secret of all time'.[8] The stated aim of the project was to harness atomic energy for peaceful purposes; and that claim was no deception. Indira Gandhi hoped the tragic day would never come when such instruments would be turned to warlike purposes, and she and her country strove consistently to secure the international mastery which could alone forbid the final catastrophe. She, like her father before her and her son Rajiv after her, worked for that end. If the great cause faltered, it was not India's fault; and when it was most hopefully revived, India took the lead.

Such were the justifications for their action which Indian leaders offered at the time, and their subsequent actions upheld their claims; but the suddenness of the May 1974 announcement was bound to have serious repercussions, not least in neighbouring Pakistan. The next day, President Bhutto called a press conference in Lahore to announce that 'Pakistan would never succumb to nuclear blackmail by India. The people of Pakistan would never accept Indian hegemony or domination in the sub-continent. Neither would Pakistan compromise its position on the right of the people of Kashmir to decide their own future.'[9] This last reference was a skilful manoeuvre, using the occasion to escape from the commitment to bilateral discussions on the issue of Kashmir which Bhutto had accepted at Simla. He was clearly gratified by the chance to direct the debate into fresh spheres; but he can hardly have been so surprised as he claimed by India's so-called 'nuclear blackmail'. Three years earlier he had set in motion discussions with Pakistan's own scientists which led to the establishment of the Pakistan Atomic Energy Commission in January 1972.

Bhutto's own qualms had much more to do with the influence these events might have on the great powers, and more especially the United States. He had been disappointed by the American failure, as he saw it, to back Pakistan in the conflicts with India, first in 1965 and again in the Bangladesh crisis of 1971. If Pakistan was to recover its independence altogether, and not only in the field of nuclear developments, it must seek to regain the full favour and even the direct support of the United States. Bhutto set about the task with a considerable combination of diplomatic skill and political acumen. The two men he had to deal with in the American administration were President Nixon and Secretary of State Kissinger. Bhutto believed he could persuade them that Pakistan should play a leading role in their strategic calculations for the entire area – at least as significant as the Shah's Iran, which seemed to be America's favourite ally at that moment. And his general approach worked. He went ahead, with direct aid from France, in building the reprocessing plant necessary to start the process of creating a nuclear capability. Kissinger made some public references to 'the fearsome weapons' which his country was so eager to stop spreading; individual countries must be ready to balance their own security against the peril of 'universal cataclysm'. This was not Kissinger's usual tone in dealing with these matters, but it represented a reproof none the less for the departure down the nuclear road on which Pakistan was currently embarked. The misunderstanding between the two countries, if such it was, was soon exposed by a gruff protest from Paris, the French department actually engaged in the supply of essential materials protesting that the Americans had no right to poke their noses into French affairs.

Since the American presidential elections were proceeding at the time, these frictions soon produced some even louder repercussions. Candidate Jimmy Carter called on all concerned to stop the sale or purchase of enriched nuclear fuel or reprocessing plants. Bhutto, who was also engaged in an election of his own, protested with some vehemence that Dr Kissinger had assured him that all these details could be disposed of in private – 'We will negotiate, we will discuss, we will talk.' No doubt all that was true; but soon the election result had deprived Bhutto of the advice of 'the man who understood him'.

Thus, amid some confusion about the rights of individual states in these nuclear matters, Pakistan set off on the nuclear race, with a particular blessing from an up-and-coming Prime Minister in Paris: Jacques Chirac, who had professed himself most offended by the American intervention and the less than obvious boon of a lesson in diplomacy from Henry Kissinger.[10] At one stage Bhutto made a notable prophecy of his own: 'Pakistan will have nuclear weapons, even if our people have to eat grass.'[11]

Chapter 2

Zero Options for All

Are there any reliable scientists? Or Church of England Bishops?

> Memo from Harold Macmillan, Prime Minister,
> to Charles Hill, in charge of Conservative public
> relations, 24 March 1958

Some account may be permitted or indeed required of my own predicaments about nuclear weapons. I was throughout the whole period a member of the Labour party, which was engaged in often ferocious but still honourable disputes on the great issues involved. Sometimes these disputes seemed to end, both for the party and the country at large, in bitter frustration; but more often, if less immediately, they could point the way to a new departure and a new hope. Since several of the old arguments are now emerging in a fresh guise, their recital here may offer guidance for the future.

Two leading Labour party members had given their minds to the subject ever since the revelations of the early 1950s – and what minds they were! Aneurin Bevan and Bertrand Russell constructed their creeds of democratic socialism from different sources and experiences; it was all the more notable for this that they developed a common faith and, even more so, a swift awareness that the curbing of the nuclear peril must take precedence over everything else. At one stage each seemed to be recommending a quite different course for tackling the situation, but what was still more striking was the intensity of their common conviction

– a product of their combined imagination and courage – that this was the greatest issue facing humankind and that everything else, including their own convenience or other predispositions, must be sacrificed for the purpose of addressing it. In their different fields of operation, each staked his whole reputation; and, momentarily at least, each seemed to lose. They behaved as reckless gamblers are supposed to do in extremity, but the counters they were playing with were the latest contrivances of the new nuclear world. To see two such minds operating at close quarters was unforgettable. At first, as I have said, they seemed to contradict each other; but in fact it was not so.

Bevan and Russell had responded in similar ways to the combined military and diplomatic events of the early 1950s. Each was among the first to recognize that the new weapons altered the terms of the entire debate and that the predominately American-inspired direction of developments in the Cold War between the superpowers was becoming speedily out of date. A British policy which took so little account of these changes was both an anachronism and a fresh menace all on its own. Looking back, these dangers must seem evident enough; but it was Aneurin Bevan who exposed them at the time in a series of major interventions and revelations. He could hardly touch on any theme of foreign policy without referring to the dark nuclear cloud which hung over all these proceedings. He had done so in March 1955, in that famous last debate in which Churchill participated, when they shared the truly big idea of stopping the nuclear arms race before it started. Throughout the Suez debates of 1956, when the futility or stupidity of the British government might itself have been thought a sufficient subject for indictment, he constantly returned to the larger perils threatening the whole planet. Most memorable of all in this sense was the speech he delivered in Trafalgar Square in November 1956, at the climax of the Labour campaign against the Suez adventure. As the crowds gathered in the square, news began to filter through of the Soviet army's re-entry into Budapest. Other countries might somehow acquire even bigger bombs than our own. Against such random perils, nothing would avail but the establishment of the international order which our own government had so pitiably despised and helped to dismantle.

A year later the same Aneurin Bevan made an even braver speech at the Labour party conference in Brighton. However, the tone and temper and emphasis of what he said were so much altered that he was accused of having changed his mind and his policy on the great question. Nothing of the sort had happened; if anything, he was even more conscious than before how heavy were the burdens which rested on the shoulders of political leaders in the nuclear age. His own beloved Labour party, which had shown a new stature and fighting spirit in the Suez debates, might soon have to take decisions of even graver consequence for the world at large, and he himself might be the new Foreign Secretary called upon to play the leading role in the exercise. It would be a tragedy indeed, not merely for himself but for the cause of world peace, if that opportunity were cast aside through some failure on the part of his party and his country. This was what he feared from the proposals which appeared on the party conference agenda, many of them backed by his own friends and allies in previous contests. This was at the root of the alarm which he expressed in the phrase about not being sent 'naked into the conference chamber'. The speech was never, in his mind, as the most vulgar reports sought to suggest, a brandishing of the nuclear bomb – as if it could ever be used for such a purpose.

It was an appeal from both heart and mind for his Labour party to appreciate how, to win the greatest prize, they must exercise a more far-seeing political judgement. He was not asking anyone to abandon his views on the wickedness or futility of nuclear weapons. He was asking for time for his Labour party to show how it could shape a policy and a government to match the demands of the new challenge. At such a moment in our history a truly great Foreign Secretary, such as Bevan would have been, could have revived the idea of stopping the world-wide nuclear race before it proceeded any further.

At first, and indeed over a period of some years, Bertrand Russell's response to the developing nuclear peril was not so very different from Bevan's. One was a practising politician, the other a practising philosopher who indeed had helped to instruct Bevan in his form of logical positivism. They shared the same temperament, satisfied only when principles were speedily translated into action. Each was among the first to recognize that the news from the Bikini tests, especially when garbled by the American authorities, seemed to threaten fresh perils of an entirely new nature. Each reacted with an almost uncannily identical attitude to the claims from Washington and Moscow that absolute right rested with their side in the argument, and that nothing but absolute allegiance to their doctrine would be tolerated. On the American side, this was the so-called Dulles doctrine, named after their most powerful Secretary of State, which had the special defect of making life impossible for would-be neutral countries like India and pushing them against their will into the Soviet camp. On the Soviet side, the even more grievous corollary was that all signs of defection from their camp in the contest – as in Hungary in 1956 – must be stamped out by military force. The Red

Army's re-entry into Budapest was a proof of what terrible risks our rulers might take in this unknown new world of nuclear perils but it also offered an indication – since the Soviet leaders did make an effort to communicate with their Western counterparts at the moment of crisis – of how a safer world might be constructed from the wreckage. Nineteen fifty-six – the passing moment which witnessed the combined crimes of Suez and Budapest – offered a special illustration of how the world's leaders could fatally misinterpret the message from their opponents. It was a central proposition of communist doctrine that Britain would always act in conformity with the grand strategy of the United States. When Britain started dropping bombs on Egypt in apparent defiance of American wishes, the Soviets guessed that this must be a ruse but determined not to be deceived. They sought a more intelligible explanation of what had happened. It must be the first strike in the war which the capitalist world was preparing against them, and their response must be sufficiently prompt and fierce. Thus the horrors and guessing games of the Cold War became intertwined with the challenge of the new nuclear age.

Russell faced these problems of the decade most comprehensively in his *Common Sense and Nuclear Warfare*, published in 1959. The temper in which he wrote and the special application of his suggested remedies were indicated in his preface, which expressed a truly individual Russell doctrine but none the less prepared the way for the comprehensive remedies which alone would constitute a sufficient response to the crisis, above all the construction of an international authority to manage nuclear power. The preface still retains its limpid force.

The aim of this book is to show possible means of achieving peace in ways which should be equally acceptable to Communist Nations, to NATO Nations and to uncommitted Nations. It is my hope that there is no word in the following pages suggesting a bias towards either side. What my opinions are concerning the merits of Eastern and Western political and economic systems, I have often stated, but opinions on these issues are not relevant in discussion of the dangers of nuclear warfare. What is needed is not an appeal to this or that -ism, but only to common sense. I do not see any reason why the kind of arguments which are put forward by those who think as I do should appeal more to one side than to the other or to Left-Wing opinion more than to that of men of conservative outlook. The appeal is to human beings, as such, and is made equally to all who hope for human survival.[1]

Both before and after the publication of this brilliantly explicit document – a new testament for the new age – Russell found himself in terrible trouble, not at all of his own making. Maybe it was his rebellious past or his rebellious future which denied him a fair hearing at the time when he deserved it most. Leave aside all these elaborate debates about future international authorities, was he not proposing that Britain must give up its bomb and leave itself defenceless? Was this not a reincarnation of the pacifist Russell of the First World War or the equivocating patriot of the Second? In actual fact, he had never been a fully fledged pacifist and his anti-fascist record was impeccable. And, according to the jargon of the day, he was not, first and foremost, a unilateralist as far as Britain's bomb was concerned. Britain's eagerness to produce the bomb he regarded as a piece of nationalist futility. He was much more concerned by the heightening tension between the two nuclear camps and how feebly, on so many occasions,

British influence was exerted to mitigate it. Nuclear weapons presented a challenge of an entirely novel kind and humankind's response must be no less original.

Common Sense and Nuclear Warfare was the document which stated Russell's case most deliberately and comprehensively, but it was by no means his first public intervention on the subject. He had taken several initiatives earlier which might have been expected to have brought forth an immediate response, but which for one reason or another had failed to do so. He delivered a BBC radio broadcast on 'Man's Peril' on 29 December 1954 in which he had referred to the possibility of 'the extermination of life on our planet'. A few months later he received an enthusiastic letter of support from Albert Einstein, and on Russell's initiative a public meeting was arranged on 9 July 1955 at the Caxton Hall in London. Here it was the scientists who seemed to speak most authoritatively; on that occasion most notably in the person of Professor Joseph Rotblat, the English physicist who had refused to continue working on the American bomb. It was Rotblat and Russell who together came up with the idea that a special effort must be made to establish contact among the top scientists, wherever they might be working, for whichever military establishments. At one stage it looked as if New Delhi might be the best place for such a meeting, thanks to the enthusiastic welcome for the idea from Indian scientists and, especially, from Prime Minister Nehru. However, transport difficulties ruled India out, and the venue eventually chosen was Pugwash, Nova Scotia. Indelibly, albeit not immediately, Pugwash had bestowed upon it an entirely new fame. That conference in July 1957, and the ensuing series of others held across the planet in even more outlandish places, seemed to be engaged in activities as novel and dangerous as the nuclear weapons themselves. Scientists of all nations were talking to one another, and the multifarious secret services of their countries were working overtime to report their activities. For this extraordinary evolution credit is due – and should never be denied – to the three chief conspirators: Russell, Rotblat and indeed Nehru, who had thought that his New Delhi was the place to give the lead.

For many of us of that period and generation, it was the Campaign for Nuclear Disarmament which best expressed the combined response which the human race must make to the bomb: the moral outrage that such an instrument should ever have been invented, the awareness that a new kind of politics would be needed to bring it under control, the determination to act together at once, whatever the cynics or the sceptics might say. It was for us the novelty of the weapons involved, plus the evidence of the lingering torture which radiation could inflict, which gave the main impetus to the campaign. Nothing so evil had ever been allowed to happen in our world before. It remained a mystery why the truth about the crimes committed at Hiroshima and Nagasaki had not percolated to the outside world. Those names should have been burned indelibly into the world's consciousness before Aldermaston or Sellafield or Chernobyl.

Since the Campaign – the notorious CND – did change the political atmosphere world-wide and not merely in isolated Britain, some competing claims were made about its origin. Two important meetings of the individuals concerned took place in 1958, the first in February in the offices of Kingsley Martin at the *New Statesman*, and the second at the offices of Canon Collins at 2 Amen Court, St Paul's. All those present were haphazardly invited. The first gathering was inspired primarily by the articles which had just appeared in the *New Statesman* by Bertrand Russell and J. B.

Priestley. The second was more representative and designed more specifically to consider some form of future organization. James Cameron of Bikini fame was there, as was Peggy Duff, destined to be the linchpin of the new group. I was there representing *Tribune*, which had already played a leading part in reporting the general H-bomb debates in the country and in particular the Labour party's Brighton controversies of 1957. The two foremost spokesmen for the case, who had already presented it with tremendous effect, were Russell and Priestley. A difference of emphasis might be detected between them. Russell gave the impression that he was less interested in the so-called 'British bomb' than in the international case for abolition of all bombs. Yet he himself had in one of his articles referred to the British nuclear programme as 'a frivolous exercise in national prestige': enough, one might conclude, to tip the balance in favour of the domestic campaign to 'ban the bomb'. However, on this aspect of the matter it was Priestley's argument which settled the debate and indeed infused the whole campaign. In his first *New Statesman* article on the subject, he had addressed the British people. In particular, he had pictured them like 'rabbits waiting for the massacre' and told them how they must 'cease to mumble and mutter, and lead the way to nuclear sanity. Alone, we defeated Hitler and alone we can defy this nuclear madness into which the spirit of Hitler seems to have passed, to poison the world.' Somehow, in the 1940s, Priestley had expressed the patriotism of the British people in their war for freedom better than anyone else. It was no small achievement to invoke the same spirit in the 1950s. What our country could do here and now to save the world became the essential test.

I expressed my ideas on the subject in an article in *CND News* in August 1964. The independent commotion created by CND was part of the way history was made. Here was how I thought the debate looked then.

> It may be instructive to consider for a moment what would have happened over these past six or seven years or what would be the situation now if there had been no Campaign for Nuclear Disarmament, no CND, in existence at all. Aldermaston would denote nothing much more than a disfigured Berkshire village. The road via Reading, Maidenhead and Slough to Turnham Green would not be stamped on the minds of some thirty or forty thousand citizens of this country with its full indelible ugliness. The decadence of modern youth could not be attributed to its distaste for committing mass murder or, rather, its insistence on stressing the point so shamelessly to its elders. The Defence White Papers of 1957 and 1958 might still be considered masterly essays in strategic doctrine. Massive retaliation might still be regarded as a respectable idea. That, in case you've forgotten, is what we pledged ourselves to do to the Russians in certain circumstances and it would be wrong to make any accusation of betrayal; the pledge has never been withdrawn. But to continue. Without CND, would the Labour Party have atrophied? Scarborough would have remained just another seaside resort. Life for Labour leaders would have been almost cushy . . . The awkward, hypothetical questions are endless.
>
> Yet even without the answers it is possible to make one modest, indisputable assertion. Without CND, the world-wide debate about the most perilous invention in history would have been less noisy, less extensive, less widespread across so many frontiers. It might, so opponents could argue, have been more clear-headed, more well-conceived, less acrimonious, less hysterical. Even if these unwarrantable claims are conceded, the other test remains. Is this a debate in which everyone should join or is it one to be left to the experts, the scientists who know, the military advisers, the

very few? The differing responses to that question go to the root of our democracy and our political system. This was appreciated by many who joined CND and was another reason for its appeal.

It may be that the statesmen would have worked to secure a test ban treaty with no less earnestness if there had been none of the pressure which CND helped to exert. It may be that for the six years prior to the signing of the treaty all the signatories who subsequently rejoiced at the banishment of the radiation and other horrors involved in testing were as secretly alarmed as CNDers and were merely suppressing or distorting the facts out of an excessive and misplaced consideration for the tender feelings of the public.

But again one simple assertion cannot be contested. The anti-CNDers, however sweeping or brash their protests, cannot deny that CND forcefully introduced into the debate an element which almost everybody else wanted to keep out. CND insisted that, whatever else the question also was, it was a *moral* one. And who will dare say that this emphasis is wrong? How debasing and dishonourable to the human species it would have been if the question of massive extermination on a scale far exceeding anything known even in Hitler's death camps had been permitted to continue being discussed without the issue of moral responsibility arising. But that is what so many people wanted and still want. CND was never guilty on that charge.

And this brings us to the most explosive point involved, CND's distinctive contribution, the demand for unilateral action by Britain. As it happened, at the first meeting when the organisation was formed in February 1958, it was by no means certain that this clause would be included in CND's programme. Some of those present at the meeting argued that the case for general nuclear disarmament should be presented in more widely-embracing terms. No doubt a few worth-while public meetings could have been conducted in this style. The Archbishop of Canterbury would doubtless have bestowed his blessing from the outset and might even have marched from Aldermaston in such a respectable cause – if there had been any marches. No one can deny the plain fact. CND developed differently from the campaigns that had gone before, provoked furious enthusiasms and enmities, and made a spectacular appeal particularly to the young precisely because it did not take refuge in vague generalities, precisely because it did urge that something could be done, precisely because it did pin responsibility on our country, on us.

This is not the place to press the case. Whatever the verdict CND has already one achievement to its credit of which many of us are extremely proud. It made our country the most active and vocal in the world in attempting to rouse mankind to an awareness of the nuclear horror. Without CND, the complacency of those in power would have been even more perilous and contemptible than it was. But, of course, this was only a first, minor victory. The armour-plated smugness of our rulers was only dented. At the moment of writing – 1964 – the most widely accepted bromide of our statesmen (disseminated by the same people who pretended to favour general disarmament and still put forward plans allegedly designed to serve this end at Geneva) was that the balance of terror keeps the peace and can always be relied on to do so. Nuclear weapons, it seems, have conferred on suffering humanity the matchless boon of perpetual peace. No one advanced this insanity with greater assurance than our own Prime Minister, Harold Macmillan. Which was just another reason why if there were no CND, it would be necessary to invent it.[2]

It was sometimes mistakenly supposed that for one reason or another Macmillan took a more liberal view of these questions than many of his Cabinet colleagues, but his private incitements to his minister of propaganda, Charles Hill, indicate a different approach.

It is most important that we should find some way of organ-
ising directly an effective campaign to counter the current
agitation against the country's possession of nuclear
weapons ... Can we persuade some influential publicists to
write articles? Are there any reliable scientists? Or Church
of England Bishops? Will you please look into this question
in consultation with the Conservative Central Office, and
let me have a report as soon as possible?

When Hill actually reported that he had recruited help in
the theological field, Macmillan noted: 'This is good.'[3] It
was easier, it seems, to find reliable theologians than reliable
scientists.

However the argument may have been influenced or
determined, we did have the right in democratic Britain to
return to the subject. And return to it we did – notably in
the 1983 general election, fought partly on this topic, which
I must be permitted to recall. For reasons which need to
be described, the great issue itself was somewhat blurred.
In the intervening years we had had a Labour government
in Britain, of which I was a member. Only a few of us in
that Cabinet had previously been full supporters of the
Campaign for Nuclear Disarmament. If we had sought,
while in office, to raise the issue in the terms of that campaign, we would not have had a chance. Such a question,
with such ramifications, must be fairly presented to the
British electorate in a general election. However, this did
not absolve us from facing fresh aspects of the problem as
they arose and seeing what contribution a Labour government might make to its containment. We did indeed do so.
The United Nations Special Session on Disarmament in
1978 offered a particular opportunity, and the Labour
government's disarmament proposals presented there by
two old-time disarmers, Philip Noel-Baker and Fenner

Brockway, outlined what comprehensive protections a real disarmament scheme could secure for all nations, great and small. But this and every other kind of protection looked like being swept aside, as in so many previous arms races, by the peremptory demands of the latest form of weaponry. Each of the so-called superpowers had piled up huge stocks of intercontinental missiles of which they claimed to keep full and final control, but now they or their satellites had produced a whole new stock of weapons with a lesser range and with final control over them inevitably diminished. The military experts or their scientific advisers in the United States and in the Soviet Union had produced variations of these products at roughly the same time and a fierce competition seemed to arise in the various satellite nations in the early 1980s as to whether it was safer to have them or to ban them. Fortunately for all concerned, that fine point was never put to the test.

One observer of these scenes put the case with a special force and authority. He was Solly Zuckerman, the official scientific adviser to the British government, but one who would never subdue the intellectual force of his argument to suit anybody. In his *Nuclear Illusion and Reality*, published in 1980, he defined the nuclear arms race at its most perilous:

For it is the man in the laboratory, not the soldier or sailor or airman, who at the start proposes that for this or that reason it would be useful to improve an old or devise a new nuclear warhead; and if a new warhead, then a new missile; and, given a new missile, a new system within which it has to fit. It is he the technician, not the commander in the field, who starts the process of formulating the so-called military need. It is he who succeeded over the years in equating, and so confusing, nuclear destructive power with

military strength, as though the former were the single and
a sufficient condition of military success. The men in the
nuclear weapons laboratories of both sides have succeeded
in creating a world with an irrational foundation, on which
a new set of political realities has in turn had to be built.
They have become the alchemists of our time, working in
secret ways that cannot be divulged, casting spells which
embrace us all.[4]

Somehow or other we had to translate these anxieties
and perils into the material for an election contest. It wasn't
easy, but the challenge was not shirked. The manifesto on
which the Labour party fought the 1983 election was once
described by Gerald Kaufman as 'the longest suicide note
in history'; the witticism certainly hit home and lived on.
A brilliant wisecrack or a piece of gossip may somehow
survive better than a good record: note the case of King
Alfred and the cakes. Most of the arguments on these
nuclear questions on which we fought lived on too. And
most of the case which we presented still stands.

One-sided disarmament; throwing away the nation's
defence; playing the Russians' game – these were the easy
charges incessantly levelled at us, repeated in almost every
newspaper, rammed home on radio and television programmes. Occasionally, some subtle elaborations on this
first theme might be attempted. Had not the great deterrent
kept the peace in Europe for thirty-odd years or more? And
while 'the nuclear umbrella' offered such sure protection
in Europe in this period, had there not been something like
140 wars elsewhere on our stricken planet, and was this not
a proof of the efficacy of nuclear weapons? Why should
such a shield be discarded? And, furthermore, was it not
evident that multilateral disarmament was the safe and
proper course to peace? Were not those who worked in

this direction the real disarmers, the real peace-makers? These arguments made up a useful case with which to exploit the combined fears and hopes of an election campaign, especially since Conservative Central Office had taken the precaution of using large chunks of taxpayers' money to launch and reiterate the same case over the previous months. The Tory Defence Secretary at the time, Michael Heseltine, claimed that the defeat of CND was the proudest achievement of his political career, a comment no doubt prompted by his exertions of this period. Yet these simplicities added up, in my view, to a great deception; a deception, moreover, on a question of supreme significance for the human race. No trifling matter, election or no election.

The first requirement was to unmask the deep complacency of the Tory case. 'As a military man who has given half a century of active service,' said Earl Mountbatten of Burma,

> I say in all sincerity that the nuclear arms race has no military purpose. Wars cannot be fought with nuclear weapons, their existence only adds to our perils because of the illusions which they have generated. There are powerful forces around the world who still give credence to the old Roman precept – if you desire peace, prepare for war. *This is absolute nuclear nonsense*, and I repeat it is a disastrous misconception to believe that by increasing the total uncertainty, one increases one's own certainty.[5]

But Earl Mountbatten's brave warning had been uttered quite a time ago – on 11 May 1979, to be exact. Between then and the time of the election in 1983, the international scene had darkened on every side. When he spoke, or at least a little while earlier, it could still be claimed that the nuclear arms race was held in check. The dangers were huge and, in a literal sense, incalculable; but some of the attitudes and the actions of the superpowers and their supporters showed an appreciation of their magnitude. The United Nations Special Session on Disarmament in 1978 offered a vista of hope and a real, well-judged and widely supported plan for moves towards multilateral disarmament. All of us in the Labour government of that time, and in the wider Labour movement in those years, knew that this plan was so ambitious that it might be derided as utopian. But we also took account of what was wisely said by some of its principal sponsors, especially those already mentioned, Philip Noel-Baker and Fenner Brockway. Their voices and arguments carried weight among the non-aligned nations whose legitimate fears were also rising year by year. And we knew that these longer-term concerns need not conflict with the achievement of the immediate next steps.

At the time when Mountbatten spelt out his warning, the second Strategic Arms Limitation Treaty had long been under negotiation and was soon to be ratified. Many experts, including President Carter's advisers in the United States, thought that there now existed something like parity in nuclear weapon power between the United States and the Soviet Union, and that this recognition could provide the basis for real reductions on both sides. Why had all those hopes been dashed? Why, since then, had the world-wide stage been so tragically transformed? To this obvious question, the orthodox Tory answer was that Soviet actions and Soviet actions *alone* – the invasion of Afghanistan, the installation of the intermediate-range SS-20 missiles in western Russia, the clampdown on Poland – were responsible for the change. No fair observer could doubt that

Soviet actions had contributed to the worsening situation but, to put the counter-argument at its lowest, who could deny that, in the nuclear field especially, there had been contributory actions on the other side: the refusal of the US Congress to ratify SALT II, President Reagan's raucous election campaign, the attempted introduction of the MX missile system? Reagan had been elected on the claim that a huge and direct military response capability was required to counter Soviet superiority; and throughout his presidency, despite all diversions and distractions, he could usually be relied upon to return to that theme.

The main British interest was to get this nuclear arms race between the superpowers – but soon to spread among many lesser powers too – back under some control, back under international supervision; to find the means whereby we could act together with as many as possible of these lesser powers who had the same paramount interest in stopping the proliferation. Yet on this aspect of the argument, the complacency of the Tory case merged into something even worse: a provocation to other parties and other countries to make their own contribution to the race, thus accelerating and intensifying it. Consider the contrast between what had allegedly happened beneath the European 'nuclear umbrella' – comforting, Chamberlainite instrument for our protection – and what had been happening in the benighted world beyond: the thirty-eight years of nuclear-guarded peace on our continent, compared with those 140 wars of varying degrees of deadliness since 1945 across the rest of the planet. How could these contrasts be comprehended by political leaders and their followers in other lands?

Campaigners for nuclear disarmament, particularly in Britain, had often been accused of nurturing insular, not to say parochial, illusions. Was there ever so constricted a piece of nationalist prejudice, so inordinate an absurdity, as the faith peddled by the British government of the early 1980s that other peoples would accept the Western case, and never draw any comparable deductions for themselves, deductions with a lethal inference? If the nuclear umbrella kept off the rain so well in Western Europe, why not in Asia, Africa, the Indian sub-continent and everywhere else? If it was an absolute necessity for Britain's future security that we should have newly perfected nuclear weapons into the 1990s and beyond, to assure us an umbrella of our own, why could not other countries say the same? Many of them – Israel and Egypt, say – treasured their independence and territorial integrity no less than we treasured ours, and perhaps with some justice felt themselves more peremptorily threatened. Some of them – China and India among them – had a new-found national pride and a scientific skill to produce the new weapons which could be set beside our own. As we have seen, India was in this context the country confronted with the most excruciating choice. Already Indians lived beneath the shadow of China's nuclear power. Could they hold back, if Pakistan went ahead? Of course not. And yet, was an Indian government to be pushed into the race, forced to accept all the consequences and inescapable economic burdens for its people, and the ever-intensifying possibility of war itself? What moral should be drawn by all the rulers of Asia, if they took seriously the Tory electoral claims? Why should they not all demand deterrent power to protect their way of life?

There was no answer to all these questions – except the one which spells universal destruction. The case for the deterrent launched afresh by the Conservative electoral machine in 1983 was, for a start, a prescription for tearing up the Non-Proliferation Treaty of 1970, one of the few measures of collective intelligence taken by the human race in the nuclear age, one of the few signs that the superpowers could be made to acknowledge an overriding common interest. Who could believe that the further proliferation of these weapons would help to preserve the peace? Who could believe that if the process continued, they would not fall into the hands of some Dr Faustus or Dr Strangelove, some new Idi Amin or new General Galtieri? Who would believe that there was no danger of that greater monstrosity even than a deliberate war – a nuclear accident with inconceivable consequences?

One of the few glimmers of common sense from spokesmen of the superpowers was that they did not dismiss the possibility of such an accident. President Reagan had written letters to Moscow about it. President Brezhnev talked about it to Denis Healey and myself when we visited Moscow in 1981. Here was a flickering light of sanity in the nuclear madhouse; and it was all the more necessary to prevent it being snuffed out when one recalled the evidence of the foremost nuclear scientists. Lord Zuckerman was no more a unilateralist than President Reagan; but he described for us the ruthless, reckless momentum which can captivate scientists in the nuclear laboratories, and which can in turn, in the boardroom of the military–industrial complexes of East and West, provide the uncontrollable push over the next precipice. Who, in the face of such evidence, could deny that nuclear arms proliferation was incomparably the greatest enemy of us all?

This was the plainest truth about our world. I felt that the whole temper of the 1983 Tory election campaign, even more than their direct commitment to deploy American cruise missiles and proceed with Trident, was a denial of it. And a special touch of cant was added with the plea that the Tories were the true disarmers, the ever-eager champions of genuine multilateral disarmament. That protestation was false in every syllable. As recently as the previous December a series of proposals for moves towards a nuclear freeze, including tentative steps towards nuclear disarmament, had been put forward at the First Committee of the United Nations. One of these, proposed by Mexico and Sweden, was approved by 119 votes; Britain, along with most of the other NATO countries, voted against it. Presumably we had taken this course to gratify our ally, the United States. No other good reason could be discerned. For the Mexican–Swedish resolution, like a similar one proposed by India – which Britain also opposed – was framed not to commit the signatories absolutely but rather to set the disarmament process in cautious motion.

Nor had this been the full extent of Britain's shame and folly. A long series of other resolutions was passed at that meeting of the UN in December 1982 on a range of matters covering test bans and nuclear-free zones. Britain either voted against or abstained on no fewer than twenty-eight of them. Just to select one at random, Mexico's resolution 'reaffirmed the conviction that a treaty banning all nuclear test explosions by all states for all time constituted a vital element for the success of efforts to prevent both vertical and horizontal proliferation of nuclear weapons, and a contribution to nuclear disarmament, and urged all states that had not yet done so to adhere forthwith to the 1963 partial Test Ban Treaty'. One hundred and twenty-four states had voted for that resolution; nineteen abstained, and two voted against – the United States and the United Kingdom. No one in our country had taken much notice of these votes; they had not been reported at all until I took the precaution of getting them recited in an article in *The Times*. I had read about them first in the columns of the *New York Herald Tribune*, where a few critical comments from UN commentators in New York were recorded, but they could not be expected to be too excited or surprised. Since May 1979 the Thatcher government had shown not the slightest, not even the most casual interest in such matters. At the Special Session on Disarmament of the United Nations in 1982 the interest shown by our government was markedly less than had been shown by its predecessors at the previous comparable meeting in 1978. It might be insisted that the more important and immediate moves towards real nuclear disarmament were concentrated at Geneva, in the talks about strategic or intermediate weapons, and especially in the discussions which came to dominate the disarmament scene – the talks about cruise and Pershing missiles. Had not the British government done its best to help forward these developments? Again, the correct answer was the exact opposite. At the precise moments when British influence might have counted, when we might have thrown our weight into the scales, the British government had done nothing.

Once the so-called zero option for some of these missiles – no new intermediate-range nuclear weapons to be allowed, and all the old ones to be withdrawn – became accepted as the goal of the negotiations, the fight to secure it was misreported. During the pre-election months – say, from about March onwards – some ignorant visitor from Mars might have supposed that President Reagan (with Mrs Thatcher's ardent support) had fought his 1980 election campaign with the zero option firmly enshrined on his banner, and on the plea that talks must be opened urgently with the Soviet Union at Geneva or anywhere else President Brezhnev cared to specify. But it had never been quite like that. President Reagan fought his Republican campaign on the demand that the United States' military budgets must make good the grievous gap which the negligent, near-traitorous Democrats had allowed to develop between America's military spending and that of the Soviet Union. No mention had been made of talks with the Soviet leaders who, as a bunch of liars, could not be trusted anyhow. No one, indeed, had ever heard then of any zero option, real or phoney.

The world had waited in vain through the whole Thatcher epoch, through 1979, 1980 and most of 1981, for new disarmament proposals to come. President Reagan said nothing on the subject, so Mrs Thatcher said nothing too. The demand for talks at Geneva or elsewhere came from Europe, from the sometimes derided 'peace movement', from the Labour party (the first body to organize a massive anti-cruise demonstration in Hyde Park on 2 June 1980), from the Social Democratic party in Germany and from Helmut Schmidt, the German Chancellor at that time, whose influence had perhaps at last tipped the balance. The zero option itself, with its idea of removing the Soviet SS-20s and their real or prospective counterparts in the West, had first been proposed by socialists and socialist parties in Europe. Denis Healey and myself, when we were in Moscow in September 1981, backed the real zero option before Mrs Thatcher or the US negotiators had learned to bowdlerize the term for their own purposes. We even got from the Russians a statement of their readiness to reduce the number of SS-20s – and they had many fewer then than they had by 1983 – only to find all such propositions derided or dismissed by a British government which had made none of its own. A few days after our return from Moscow, President Reagan used the actual words in a slightly different context. The term had at least – and at last – acquired respectability. It was freely used by the same Douglas Hurd, now a minister, who as an under-secretary at the Foreign Office had been so ready to denounce us in the early 1960s.

All through that period, from the last days of the Carter administration when, alas, the US government was allowed to abandon the attempt at ratification of SALT II without a cheep of protest from official quarters in Britain, right through to early 1983, the Thatcher policy on all these aspects of international affairs was to accept the Reagan policy. Nothing more; nothing less; never by any accident, much less by design, anything more original, ambitious or imaginative. There was just one occasion when a British Foreign Secretary dared to speak out of turn in response to an overture from the East – the exception which proves the rule. Francis Pym, when Foreign Secretary, welcomed as 'constructive' the proposal which the new Soviet leader, Yuri Andropov, made at the so-called Prague Summit in January 1983, in blazing contrast to the Prime Minister's reaction to the same Andropov proposals the previous December, which Mrs Thatcher rejected in an answer in the House of Commons even before she had allowed herself the chance to hear what they were. Thereafter, Mr Pym resumed his silence on this topic. Such was the beginning and end of any honourable or even noticeable part played by the British government in assisting the pressure for disarmament in any field whatsoever.

The British government of that day and its apologists also applied their complacent tone and attitude to the issue of cruise missile deployment. Why all the fuss? asked *The Times*. Why had these weapons assumed 'a symbolic importance'? For 'cruise', we were assured, 'is no more or less of a doomsday weapon than any other nuclear systems in the armouries of NATO and the Warsaw Pact'. So why worry? But then *The Times* had added an even more ineffable touch. 'Indeed, the cruise is functionally the successor of the F-111 aircraft which is a familiar sight over East Anglia . . .'[6] I tried to remember; the last time I recalled being offered such cool, scientific comfort was on that same visit to Moscow when the Russians explained to Denis Healey and myself that the SS-20s were not really a new weapon system at all but just a functional adjunct to what had gone before.

Yet, in continued defiance of the wisdom of the superpowers, whose favourite claims so frequently coincide or overlap or fatally contradict each other, multitudes of people in Europe – and most other continents, I would guess – did see the proposed cruise and Pershing programmes as fresh, maybe near-incontrovertible evidence that the world was set to embark upon a new and even more dangerous stretch of the race. This supposition appears all the more justified as we recall that when the European governments accepted the cruise programme, the SALT II agreement had recently been reached and was soon to be ratified. The horizons then were not all black; the race was not all helter-skelter in one direction. But who now could offer even those modest comforts? SALT II had been torn up – in Washington, not Moscow. The fitful hopes of 1978 had been dashed by the fiascos of 1982 and 1983. The world could be blown up by functional adjuncts more powerful than the bomb dropped on Hiroshima.

But let us revert to our alleged illusions. Campaigners for nuclear disarmament set too much store, it was suggested, by the notion that nuclear-free countries – should we ever attain our ideal – would offer less inviting targets to our enemies, or that other countries would follow our example, or that the Soviet government would never use its huge military power for purposes of blackmail. But none of these was the real foundation of the disarmament case. If the nuclear holocaust comes, it is doubtful whether anyone will ever know where the deepest guilt will lie. The real case for nuclear disarmament rested on a truth more profound than any which the Tory electioneers dared to state or debate or challenge. The extermination will be shared by us all, nuclear or non-nuclear, blackmail or no blackmail, umbrella or no umbrella.

Consider how vast had been the enlargement of the military machines in this terrible race over the forty-odd years of glorious European peace (during which, incidentally, no small part of the 140 wars among God's lesser breeds elsewhere had been caused by the miniature arms races sponsored and sustained by European, American and Soviet arms sales). Consider how the pace was now quickening. Consider how the Americans, with or without the new MX system, intended to spend more and much more than ever before. Consider how the Soviet Union might strive to match or outdo them. Such was the mountainous nature of the world crisis which faced us in May and June 1983. Many of its contours had been visible for months, even years, before. Yet with the breakdown in the relations between the superpowers, with all the accumulating and imminent dangers, no language which described the reality could be dismissed as exaggerated or alarmist. I must plead guilty to the charge that both during and before that election, ever since I had been appointed Labour leader, I had returned to the same obsession in every speech I delivered. But, of course, even among those who shared the same objectives and the same sense of urgency, the question remained: how best could we present our case and forestall what we knew would come from our opponents? That, for sure, was always a fit topic for debate or dispute.

I believed – and it required no special insight, since almost everybody with whom I discussed it concurred – that the proper way to present our agreed Labour policy for stopping the nuclear arms race was to show how it could be set in motion, step by step, stage by stage. Of course, it did *not* mean throwing away our defences. Of course, it did *not* mean that advance on all disarmament fronts could be achieved at once. Of course, it did *not* mean that Britain alone could set the pace. It *did* mean that Britain could re-establish and exert some influence in these affairs; that we could set a timetable which proved we meant business; that the work for multilateral agreements could be combined with unilateral initiatives.

So we proposed that, as one of the first steps, Britain at the United Nations should reverse the decision of the previous December and agree to a freeze on the production, deployment and testing of nuclear weapons, and to a comprehensive test ban; that, as another first step, we should make clear our refusal to site cruise missiles on our soil; and that, in addition, we should cancel the Trident programme. These steps were to be the immediate ones, but others would follow soon – steps towards a change in NATO's strategy, towards accepting the doctrine of no first use of nuclear weapons, towards finding ways in which non-nuclear zones could be established in Europe, towards the inclusion, as the negotiations proceeded, of Britain's Polaris force in the nuclear disarmament negotiations – in which Britain should participate.

A step-by-step process was what I favoured and what we actually proposed. And yet, was *any* form of unilateral action, of so called one-sided disarmament, really so out-rageous? Some experts did not think so. Lord Carver, in a notable speech in the House of Lords debate in February 1983, had approached the matter more imaginatively:

> I suggest, therefore, as I have often done before in this House, that NATO should make a radical examination of its nuclear armoury, based on the principle that it would be suicidal for the Alliance to be the first to use nuclear weapons. I believe that without any prejudice to deterrence or to its security, it could abolish nuclear artillery now; that is, nuclear warheads fired out of guns. I know of no sensible soldier who really believes that one would be able to use them in a way which could have the decisive effect their originators claimed, or who thinks he would ever get per-mission to fire before it was too late – and that, without taking into account what the enemy would fire back in retaliation. I see no reason why the decision to abolish nuclear artillery should not be a unilateral one by NATO as a whole. It would eliminate at one stroke 2000 warheads, all American, and automatically eliminate the enhanced radiation warhead, sometimes called the neutron bomb. And so long as the United States maintains longer-range systems, the threat of retaliation by them should deter the Soviet Union from using their short-range systems, if they decide to keep them. I suggest that NATO could take that step and withdraw other systems to the 250 kilometres which, as I understand it, was the recommendation of the Olaf Palme Commission, unilaterally, without prejudicing its security. But once you demand that measures must be reciprocal you get involved with verification, and negoti-ations invariably get bogged down on that.[7]

To return to the general argument about the safety of the West: was it true that we were failing to recognize the real existing balance between the great powers? William

McGeorge Bundy, formerly National Security Adviser to Presidents Kennedy and Johnson, had described the reality more objectively than some more recent spokesmen:

> Q.   But do you feel there is a situation of nuclear inequality in Europe that needs to be addressed?
>
> A.   I think that the most important measure of nuclear balance is the overall nuclear balance between the Warsaw Pact nations and NATO. And I do not think there is a great imbalance in those broader terms. The United States has between 9000 and 10,000 warheads in its strategic forces. On the Soviet side there are perhaps 2000 fewer. In terms of the ability to survive a first strike, the American force is better than the Soviet force because we have so heavily invested in more survival modes than the land-based missile. Very often the administration makes comparisons only in terms of land-based missiles, but when it does that, it is talking about three-quarters of the Soviet force and one-quarter of ours.[8]

And – not to dodge any part of the charge – had not Labour party nuclear disarmers, CNDers like myself, based their case on the outlandish hypothesis that the Russians and the Americans would follow our example? No, that had never been our claim either. Way back in the late 1950s, at the time when CND was founded, Bertrand Russell had discussed the leading question of what might be expected from the superpowers, and how they might be influenced. We may quote again from his *Common Sense and Nuclear Warfare* – published, I emphasize, in 1959; half a century ago. He included a short appendix on unilateral disarmament, from which I quote three paragraphs:

> Some of the critics have laid stress upon the fact that in certain hypothetical circumstances I should think either the

East or the West well advised if it disarmed unilaterally. My critics have omitted my provisos and have spoken as if I had advocated a disarmament policy for the West alone, and not equally for the East, in the circumstances supposed. My critics are not wholly to blame for this. I have been led into a purely academic issue as if it were one of practical politics. Everybody knows that neither the United States nor the USSR will disarm unilaterally. The question whether either would be wise to do so is therefore no more than an exercise in theoretical ethics. Speaking practically, and not theoretically, what I advocate is that methods should be sought of, first lessening the East–West tension and then negotiating agreements on vexed questions on the basis of giving no net advantage to either side. Such negotiations, if they are to be satisfactory, must include the mutual renunciation of nuclear weapons with an adequate system of inspection.

It is true that I advocate practically, and not only theoretically, the abandonment of the H-bomb by Britain and the prevention of the spread of H-bombs to Powers other than the United States and the USSR. I do not consider that unilateral renunciation of British H-bombs would have any measurable effect upon the balance of power, and I do consider that the acquisition of H-bombs by many Powers will greatly increase the danger of a nuclear war. This makes the question of British renunciation of H-bombs quite distinct from that of general unilateral disarmament by one of the two camps.

Many of my critics, though they are in the habit of proclaiming that they value freedom, on this point deceive themselves. They do not think that those who prefer life rather than death, even under Communism or under Capitalism, as the case may be, should be free to choose the alternative that they prefer. Not only the inhabitants of communist nations – or of capitalist nations – are denied by them the most elementary freedom, which is freedom to choose survival. The view that No World is better than a Communist World, or that No World is better than a Capitalist World, is one that is difficult to refute by abstract arguments, but I think that those who hold it should question their right to impose their opinion upon those who do not hold it by the infliction of the death penalty upon all of them. This is an extreme form of religious persecution, going far beyond anything that has been advocated in previous human history.[9]

The case argued by Russell on nuclear weapons was part of the broader foreign policy programme which the Labour party presented to the British electorate in 1983. It was a programme fully in accord with the best internationalist traditions of the Labour party throughout the century. We were calling for collective international action to meet the new menace. Moreover, what we were proposing had a special appeal for other countries which were seeking to use their newly established democratic institutions to build the new international order.

*

No seer, however gifted, not even an Indian one, could have foretold the deliverance which was offered to the world in the 1980s and 1990s. Several claimants might argue that theirs was the particular strategy which best pointed the way; but none of these told the whole story, and indeed, since the end-game has not been finally staged, the story is not yet finished. As in previous key periods throughout the century, India played a distinctive role, perhaps an indispensable one. Since the Western powers had so grievously missed the point before, it was not surprising, though it was no less galling for that, when they did it again.

Somehow the Americans had inherited from the British

an imperial arrogance towards India. They knew better not only what was good for themselves, but what was good for India too. Indira Gandhi objected to these displays of patronage even more than her father had, and when she resumed the premiership of India in 1980, with the support of an even larger proportion of her own people than before, she was all the more outraged to see that Pakistan was still the favoured ally of the West. We seemed to have learned nothing from the Pakistan military collapse of the 1970s or the constant reversion to dictatorial regimes in Islamabad. Perhaps American leaders preferred it that way: new dictators might be easier to deal with than new democracies, and the neo-colonialists certainly collected some extraordinary specimens in their menagerie of pliable allies, from Idi Amin to the Shah of Iran. Indian leaders after independence often felt that their judgements on such questions of personality might be more dependable than the combined wisdom of the British Foreign Office and the American State Department. India pleaded the cases of, say, Cheddi Jagan, or Kenneth Kaunda or Michael Manley or Nelson Mandela long before these men emerged as saviours of their own countries. Their sounder instincts derived from the special brand of freedom which was developed in independent India, and which still flourished when Indira Gandhi returned to power in 1980.

Mrs Gandhi was supposed to have damned herself for ever, at least in the eyes of true freedom-lovers, by her resort to emergency powers in the mid-1970s. Some terrible events had occurred, and her apologies for them were pitifully inadequate. But, on another reckoning, the deeper the offence, the more remarkable was her recovery. Her comeback after such a defeat is unique among democratic leaders. She had not expected defeat when she called the first election of 1977 although, as the hour came closer, her doubts began to grow. When catastrophe struck her, it was worse than anyone could have imagined. It looked as if she was finished, not merely politically, but morally, almost physically. The victors pursued her and her family with a vindictiveness which can still take one's breath away. Some of the members of the new government had good reasons for hating her; but some of them had been her friends or protégés. Together, all combined to seek out legal or parliamentary devices which would ensure that neither Mrs Gandhi nor – especially – her son Sanjay would ever again play any part in Indian politics. But she faced it all with a persistent courage to confound all her accusers. She had an inner strength that, as with her father, was not in any sense religious. Like him, she had come to know and revere the diversity of cultures which India represented. Her guide at that testing moment was her love of India and the peoples of India. She spent the next four years touring every corner of the country, refreshing her confidence in them and their confidence in her. No comparable odyssey has ever been undertaken in the history of democratic politics.

By 1980 Indira Gandhi was a wiser woman; but by then, too, some of India's problems looked even more intractable. Fresh troubles threatened in Kashmir and she took prompt measures to contain them. An even more serious threat to Indian unity was posed by some Sikh extremists; to concede their demand of a separate state within India would have opened the way to the dissolution of the republic itself. To the north, disturbances in Afghanistan posed a further threat. The Soviet Union's leaders were foolish enough to suppose that a full-scale invasion was the only remedy. Mrs Gandhi could tell them that they were embarking on as hopeless a campaign as the Americans in Vietnam. But they too were mesmerized by their military power. For India, the Soviet Union's combined crime and folly inflicted a special agony; for it gave the Americans an excuse to pour fresh military resources into Pakistan.

Across the whole international scene, Mrs Gandhi was soon facing dangerous shifts which might have knocked her off balance altogether. Instead she picked her path between the giants with a new assurance and determination. The great powers had to understand, she said, 'that we are true friends only when we are not satellites'. She rubbed shoulders afresh with some other leaders when she went to Belgrade in May 1980 for the funeral of President Tito. She learned some lessons there, and could help teach them too:

> The civilisations of the West have reached a crisis point. The known systems have become outdated. They no longer operate efficiently or answer all the questions and in this I include both Capitalism and Communism as they are understood in classical terms ... The challenge of the eighties will have to be met. The great powers are still bound in the straitjacket of concepts such as balance of power and spheres of influence – the world has become much more complicated, and the gap between the rich and the poor widens every day. A country like India does not fall into their schedule.[10]

The foreign policies of India, under her guidance at least, had a consistency which deserved some acknowledgement; but it was rarely granted. When she went to the United States in July 1982, on an official visit, she was bombarded at the airport with questions about Afghanistan. Did not India's acceptance of weapons from the Soviet Union threaten to undermine India's independence? She answered promptly and fiercely: 'I still belong to a generation whose whole life was spent fighting for freedom. I cannot conceive India shadowed by another power.' That visit gave her the chance to speak privately with President Reagan. Her idea was to concentrate on the supreme question: the nuclear danger and the urgent need for world-wide disarmament. But she came away with the impression that the President was unable to concentrate his mind on the subject. Still, she could talk to others in her best plain manner, and when she returned home (having had a meeting in Moscow with an ailing President Brezhnev almost as uncomprehending as Reagan) she put the same questions to some of her intimate friends. 'Why were the Americans still destabilizing our sub-continent, still supporting Zia in Pakistan? How can we hold India together? How could they convince the United States that they are not at all against them and that their friendship could have value only if India is strong and stable in itself? The US administration did not seem to have learned anything from the countries which blindly accepted their guidance.' Piercing questions indeed; but seldom answered in the United States itself. India seemed sometimes to command a better audience elsewhere, thanks partly to Indira's leadership, which now acquired a fresh resilience. She presided with skill and justified pride over the conference of the non-aligned countries held in New Delhi in March 1983. She opened the proceedings with a clear and comprehensive warning of how nuclear weapons threatened the annihilation of the human species. She thought the Non-Aligned Movement itself had acquired a new authority and a new status. 'It is an assertion of human-kind's will to survive despite oppression, despite the growing arms race and ideological division.' Some experts chose to forget, or maybe they had never learned, that the

Non-Aligned Movement promised to expand, but always by peaceful means; and, amazingly, old enemies would sit down together. 'We had a spot of bother over Iran and Iraq,' Indira reported to a friend just afterwards. According to the dictates of the English alphabet their representatives had to sit alongside each other.

Each of us in the nuclear age may have different recollections of which particular description brought home best and most indelibly the nature of the threatened destruction, of the winter to follow. Philip Morrison, a physicist from the Massachusetts Institute of Technology, performed this service for Indira. He wrote thus:

> Nuclear strategic attacks would lead to fires on an unprecedented scale: whole cities aflame; gas and oil wells, storage tanks, and refineries burning freely; vast fires raging widespread over forest and field . . .
>
> The consequences could be apocalyptic: everywhere darkness at noon. The unprecedented quantity of black smoke spread in the winds from many hundreds of simultaneous conflagrations would form a curtain over much of the northern hemisphere in a matter of weeks. The warming rays of the sun by day could not reach the ground, but the infra-red radiation from the surface of the earth could take out the surface heat into space by day and by night.
>
> The outcome of unrelieved twilight day after day, perhaps broken now and again by brief spells of clearing, might be sudden winter within a few weeks. It would be a bizarre displaced season, carrying spells of freezing weather even where a winter never comes. By some estimates ice would form south to the flooded paddy fields near the equator. The open sea holds too much heat to cool so rapidly, and the temperature contrast could drive chains of howling rainstorms, freezing and warm by turns, across the tropical coastlines.[11]

Indira Gandhi's efforts were cut brutally short by her own destruction. At the moment of crisis in her argument with sections of the Sikh community, she was murdered in cold blood by a Sikh member of her own bodyguard. It was a terrible fate for her, and for her country. No doubt she had made misjudgements in her dealings with her Sikh compatriots; but, when some friends warned her that she should take the precaution of making changes in her bodyguard, she refused. That would be to surrender to the self-same religious intolerance which she believed could be the second most deadly threat to India's future – second only to the nuclear threat itself.

*

If my account of Indira Gandhi's contribution to the defence of Indian democracy seems too uncritical, a good corrective may be for readers to turn to Sunil Khilnani's *The Idea of India*, his brilliantly compressed but still richly judicious account of the story of independent India. He singles out as the country's outstanding – and unique – achievement the development of a genuine democracy to suit its own interest, and the way this has been accepted by the overwhelming majority of the Indian people. 'As an independent democratic state since 1947, India remains defiantly anomalous,' writes Khilnani.[12] Indira Gandhi made her own indispensable contribution to that achievement. If she had failed to accept the verdict of the electorate in 1977, or if she had failed to offer the prospect of a new democratic recovery, India would have followed the pattern of military dictatorships so common in the rest of Asia.

Chapter 3

Gorbachev's Ally

West German foreign minister Willy Brandt argued that
'the moral and political justification of a non-proliferation
treaty follows only if the nuclear states regard it as a step
towards restrictions of their own armaments and towards
disarmament and clearly state they are willing to act
accordingly.'

Lawrence S. Wittner, *Resisting the Bomb*, vol. II

Ever since the start of the Cold War in the early 1950s
a dominant aim of United States' political-cum-military
strategy – in later years, *the* dominant aim, it might be said
– was to force the pace in arms production so relentlessly
that the Soviet economy would break under the strain
before the military horror had to be unleashed. It was an
old doctrine brought up to date: if you want peace, prepare
for war, with nuclear knobs on. At the end of the 1980s,
after a period of seeming failure, it was suddenly crowned
with spectacular success. The Soviet Union collapsed. The
arms race had been pursued – contrary to most prophecies
– to its peaceful conclusion. *QED.*

However, the American theory, potent as it may seem
to be in its practical results, has some serious deficiencies.
Good for the Americans it may be; but not for the rest of
us. And that includes not only America's potential enemies,
such as the old Soviet Union or present-day China, but
faithful friends like, say, Britain and France. The American
chiefs of staff – call them what you will; Eisenhower's

'military–industrial complex' was a convenient alternative term – always took the view, right from the start of the nuclear age, that it would be safer if the secret were kept in American hands. They made a proposal, in the Baruch Plan, to place the bomb under international control. It was a good plan, and many serious international observers supported it. But it was not good enough; the Soviet leaders rejected it, and soon accepted for themselves the American logic. Whatever else happened, whatever else was sacrificed, they must acquire as quickly as possible membership of the nuclear club which provided the only safe shield. Soon some other countries, such as our own and France, took the view that we or they must have the shield too. Obviously, the Americans would not readily accept this deduction; for a while they thought that the British demand for facilities to make the bomb must be treated with caution, while the French demand could be dismissed as a piece of Gaullist perversity. But who could deny the logic? The proliferation of the weapons might be even more perilous than the race between the great powers. If Iraq got the bomb, what about its neighbours? If Israel got the bomb? Or if Israel did not? A painful choice for Israel, and for Israel's neighbours. Some time in the 1980s Israel went ahead with the programme, presumably with American approval. A little earlier, in 1981, it launched a preventive strike against Iraq's nuclear reactor at Osirak. And a little later, in 1984, the Israeli secret service conducted an extraordinary exploit on British soil when they kidnapped an Israeli citizen, Mordecai Vanunu, who was revealing to British journalists some part of Israel's secret. Such was one consequence of the American failure to establish international control over nuclear weapons: the wide spread among so many nations of the will and the capacity to make such weapons.

The other defect in the American system which produced the collapse – not so grave in its consequences as the one just mentioned but still serious – was the mistaken judgements which it implanted in the American mind about what was truly happening in the Soviet Union itself and how this might be best turned to the advantage of the Americans and the rest of the world which had made itself so dependent on American power. It was especially unfortunate that such misguided interpretations should be accepted when both America and Britain had in Moscow or elsewhere in their diplomatic service those who recommended courses which could have proved more fruitful. One such opportunity occurred just after the death of Stalin, when Churchill wanted to open discussions with his successor. Eisenhower blocked that one, presumably at the behest of his military–industrial complex before he claimed to have it under control. Another arose soon after Nikita Khrushchev's exposure of the Stalin tyranny and before the Cuban adventure. All such opportunities were dismissed because they ultimately clashed with the dominant military doctrine, which stated that the Soviet leaders, and now no doubt the Chinese leaders too, understood nothing but superior force and that nothing whatever must be allowed to stand in the way of making that predominance prevail. President Reagan, elected in 1980, made his espousal of this view superabundantly clear in a speech denouncing 'the evil empire' with which any kind of reputable diplomatic deal would be impossible. And indeed, in the last days of President Brezhnev the Soviet leader was engaged in some fresh evil enterprises, suddenly seeking to impress Poland in the West and Afghanistan in the East with his own country's superior military strength. These were deep, fresh tragedies for the peoples concerned, all the more inexcusable for their eventual futility.

President Reagan also had another military project which he hoped to add to America's already overwhelming power. It was called the Strategic Defense Initiative, and the idea was the creation of a shield which would make possible a nuclear attack without the fear of retaliation. President Reagan was so enamoured of the idea that he was moved to quote the revolutionary Thomas Paine: 'We have it in our power to start the world anew.' I sometimes thought that the appearance of a Paine quotation in a Reagan speech must be the result of a wager among Reagan's speech-writers, but here it appeared in a strange and chilling context. The arms race could be transferred to space at infinite cost and peril.

The phenomenon which not speech-writers, or military experts, or even prophetic Thomas Paine could foresee was Mikhail Gorbachev. In my estimation, he did more than any other single individual engaged in the ugly trade of world politics to make possible a peaceful ending of our war-ridden century, with the future bonus – if we would only listen carefully to his prescription – of finally lifting the shadow of the nuclear holocaust. Whatever else he was or was not, he was the most passionate nuclear disarmer who ever appeared on the planet. And he's still there helping to guide us now. In October 1996 he published a book of his memoirs which not only reflected on his past but persisted in emphasizing his prophecy for the future.[1]

Gorbachev is passionately concerned to save both his beloved Russia and the world at large. He has the right to be heard, since it was his combination of political intelligence and courage which prepared the way for the decisive changes of the 1980s and the 1990s. The account of how he had to work for the chance to speak on a national stage in the first place could have filled a volume on its own. As he fought his way up through the suffocating communist system the bureaucrats could have beaten any sense of human decency out of him, as they did with so many others. But somehow he was always making deductions of his own; from his wartime experience when his village was occupied by the Germans, from a Russian literature which gloried in a special humanity, from a noble Indian visitor to his Moscow University called Jawaharlal Nehru, who told his audience it was their duty to make a better world.

He had some special Russian words to describe what he meant by freedom, and somehow he gained for them a world-wide currency. He was shaken and ashamed by the news of the explosion at the Chernobyl nuclear power plant in 1986. The scientists and the party specialists had sustained what he called 'a spirit of servility, fawning, clannish and a persecution of independent thinkers'. Across the planet as a whole there had been 151 significant radiation leaks at nuclear power stations, but the Chernobyl crime was the worst. It gave a driving impetus to his dream of a new nuclear policy for all mankind.

Like some of his predecessors in the post of General Secretary of the Communist Party, he faced unforeseen turmoil in neighbouring states which might have wrecked any programme of reforms; but he never believed military force could be the cure, and his restraint saved the day and changed the face of Eastern Europe. He did not foresee the pace of change in Germany and made no pretence that he did, but this sudden crisis made his response to it all the more significant.

However, it was in the broader field of world-wide disarmament that he showed the truest wisdom and originality. He knew that an end to the arms race was necessary if his country was not to be destroyed. He knew how his predecessors in office, even when they started to talk peace, had often found it easier to yield to the demands of the military–industrial complex; for Moscow had its version of that deadly machine to match the one which dictated policy in Washington. Fortunately for us all, the Gorbachev who was seeking an escape from the Cold War – which could turn into a hot one overnight – found counterparts in other countries willing to respond to his overtures. He readily acknowledged those who would do business with him, and we were all the beneficiaries of that trade. But it was Mikhail Gorbachev from Moscow who set the pace and maintained the momentum.

It is a tragedy beyond measure that he no longer retains the political authority in his own country to carry through his disarmament programme. He was quite prepared for democratic reforms of the most far-reaching nature, but he could not accept the destruction of any effective federal authority in the old Soviet Union. Prophetically, he feared that such a destruction might lead to several Chechen revolts, condemning patriotic Russian soldiers to 'fight for an unjust cause and become hostages to a shameful policy'. He should have been in power to deal with the challenge of the new century. The world would be much safer if he were. But since the job was so cruelly wrenched from his hands, he has done the next best thing. He has recited the whole truth and urged us all, first and foremost his own countrymen, to face the task and follow the timetable he laid down: a world-wide disarmament plan, with all nuclear arsenals suitably destroyed.

Some other world leaders – Mrs Gandhi, for one, as we have noted – had not found it easy to talk with Reagan on these supremely important questions, for the American President could give the impression of casualness or sheer ignorance; but it was not so with Gorbachev. Their first good discussions took place at their meeting in Geneva, even before their most famous negotiations at Reykjavik, which generated the declaration 'Nuclear war cannot be won and must never be fought'[2] – making nonsense of the arms race which was still proceeding. Wherever else the argument turned, whether with President Reagan himself or his most helpful assistant, George Shultz, it was to this overriding truth that they constantly returned. Reagan, it seems, had flashes of horror when the final reality was brought home to him, by Gorbachev or anybody else. Previously, when challenged on the point, he had occasionally been alleged to answer that God would appear at his side in the hour of crisis; this may have been a comfort to some in the Bible belt of his own country, but cut little ice elsewhere. However, as Edward Luttwak revealed at the end of his reflections on the Cuba crisis quoted in chapter 1, there were moments when, in the light of some new revelation, Reagan would abandon the committed strategy of his country and NATO altogether, as if he were some new recruit on the road to Aldermaston.

When the American and Soviet leaders met on their own, some of those excluded were bound to feel suspicious. 'No more Reykjaviks' was the rumoured comment by our own Prime Minister Thatcher, reported back to Moscow. Maybe the inference was unfair. Margaret Thatcher too wanted to do business with Gorbachev, and her readiness to make that declaration had helped towards Reagan's enlightenment; but maybe it was commercial business, not nuclear matters, which she found more congenial to consider. She never seemed eager to discuss the fate of the universe. Gorbachev, though, saw a different prospect. At the time – not in some faint recollection – he wrote: 'Reykjavik mapped out a route by which humankind can regain the immortality it lost when nuclear arms incinerated Hiroshima and Nagasaki.' Such was the sense of history and political leadership needed to tackle the problem. Whatever else his critics denied him, Gorbachev possessed this wisdom in an exceptional degree.

He continued to report the debate thus:

After Reykjavik and especially after our proposal to conclude a separate agreement on medium-range missiles, the NATO circles raised a ballyhoo about the impossibility of securing peace in Europe without nuclear weapons. I had a sharp debate with Mrs Thatcher on this issue. She claimed that for Britain nuclear weapons are the sole means of ensuring its security in the event of a conventional war in Europe. This is a philosophy of doom. I told the British Prime Minister: 'When you are vowing that nuclear weapons are a blessing and that the US and the USSR may reduce their level whereas Britain will keep aloof, it becomes only too obvious that we see in front of us an ardent supporter of nuclear weapons. Let us assume that we begin the process of disarmament, remove medium-range missiles from Europe and reduce strategic offensive weapons by fifty per cent or by another percentage, while you continue building up your nuclear forces. Have you ever thought what you will look like in the eyes of world public opinion?' I thought it was my duty to recall that Britain had been a participant in the trilateral negotiations on the general and complete prohibition of nuclear tests and then it lost all interest in those negotiations. We observed a moratorium on nuclear testing for eighteen months whereas Britain did not.

The existence of nuclear weapons is fraught with a permanent risk of unpredictability. If we follow the logic that nuclear weapons are a blessing and a reliable guarantee of security, then off with the nuclear non-proliferation treaty too. Especially as dozens of states now have the scientific, technological and material capability to build their own bomb. What moral right do the current nuclear powers have to reject the same to, say, Pakistan, Israel, Japan, South Africa, Brazil or any other country? But what then would become of the world, of international relations?[3]

Some of Gorbachev's arguments with Mrs Thatcher were more pertinent for a later period; they did not imperil the negotiations with the United States on longer-term commitments on arms limitations, or the immediate acceptance of the so-called zero option for the medium-range cruise missiles which had caused such alarm in the 1980s. However, the Thatcher doctrine, if insisted upon, could have put in jeopardy some other significant checks on the nuclear race, namely the test ban and the non-proliferation treaties. It would indeed have been a most pitiable and tragic accompaniment to the larger agreement between the Soviet Union and the United States if at the same time other provisions, insufficient though they might be, had had to be abandoned. Mikhail Gorbachev's own confidence and energies might therefore have been impaired by such an outcome. He felt he had by his efforts called forth fresh support among the peoples of the nuclear powers, irrespective of the stance taken by their rulers – a point he would impertinently mention to Mrs Thatcher, not always with her approval. However, the imperfections of his relations with some political leaders made it all the more exhilarating and justly instructive when he found a country and a political leader who welcomed his initiative in the historic terms it deserved. Independent India, as we have seen, had been guided to this position by its previous far-seeing leaders. Their successor, Rajiv Gandhi, helped to secure the next stride forward towards world peace. Gorbachev never forgot what he owed to Rajiv, and nor should we.

The Delhi Declaration signed by the two leaders in New Delhi on 27 November 1986 was the most ambitious disarmament programme ever projected in the nuclear age. Along with a whole series of other measures, it proposed the total elimination of nuclear arsenals by the end of the century. It set out interim goals which could prepare the way for this final achievement: the stopping of the arms race in space, a ban on nuclear weapons tests, the destruction of all existing chemical weapons, a series of reductions in conventional forces. One party to this agreement was a nuclear power which had at last realized the perils of its capabilities. The other was a country which – thanks to the preventive measures taken by Indira Gandhi in the 1970s – would soon have the capacity to produce nuclear weapons but consistently hoped that international action would make it unnecessary to do so. Moreover, this India had a special right to appeal to some of the countries – Argentina, Greece, Mexico, Tanzania, Sweden – which had previously joined together to secure a world-wide moratorium on the testing and manufacture of nuclear weapons. And this India had a zestful youth to lead it to match its ancient wisdom. If the young Rajiv had come into his inheritance by birth and made many mistakes, it was no less true that he brought to the task a shining courage, an unshakeable good humour and a resolve to carry forward his mother's work in the establishment of India's place in the world. No one else with the power to act on our threatened planet acted so swiftly and intelligently to welcome the Gorbachev initiatives, and Rajiv's response encouraged Gorbachev to proceed. It was no small service to humanity at large.

I had the chance of seeing Rajiv in action on several occasions, public and private, and I wholeheartedly confirm Gorbachev's verdict. He might be unorthodox in his manner and his approach to public occasions, but this could be a positive sign of fitness for the new tasks of a new age. When we first met the two brothers, Sanjay and Rajiv, in action in Indira's own household, there was no attempt, nor indeed any need, to disguise Rajiv's dislike for public affairs. The favouritism which his mother showed towards Sanjay – maybe the most fateful of all her mistakes – could not have been easy to bear; but Rajiv kept his temper and his place through many trials, and when Sanjay was killed in June 1980 and Sanjay's wife could not deal with the crisis, it was Rajiv and his wife Sonia who stepped forward to save the situation in the household, as he later did in the country at large. He picked out the greatest causes which India had served and sought to serve them afresh. Among Commonwealth spokesmen he became the foremost to denounce the apartheid system in South Africa – not so easy a task for the young spokesman of India while the old imperialism still prevailed in South Africa and while Britain's Prime Minister was still denouncing Nelson Mandela as a terrorist. But he was most insistent of all in his efforts to secure progress on disarmament, some sign of real action on the Delhi Declaration. In 1988, two years after it was first proclaimed, the Delhi Declaration was translated into the proposals which Rajiv made in India's name at the meeting of the United Nations General Assembly. He called for 'a ban on the use, production and testing of nuclear weapons and freezing of existing stockpiles as well as the destruction of nuclear weapons under international safeguards and inspection by AD 2010'. The slight extension of the date of deliverance by a decade from the end of the century was not a sign of weakness, but rather an attempt to prove how serious the proposal was. Once more the members of the original nuclear club, with the notable exception of Mikhail

Gorbachev, failed to respond to the repeated arguments of those who were outside it.

So little did the British government in particular seem to care about the implications of lesser arms races that it disclaimed any responsibility for intervening, even when the principles of the Non-Proliferation Treaty became implicated. Advisers on the subject in the Indian defence department detected – not for the first time – evidence that Pakistan was moving towards a fresh stage in its preparation of a nuclear capacity. If that next step was taken, India would not be able to hold back. Much the best move for India and everybody else would be for major strides to be taken towards the ideal of the Delhi Declaration, but an Indian government which allowed Pakistan to steal a march on it in these nuclear matters would invite serious political retribution. I reported the conversation I had with Rajiv on this subject as faithfully as I could to Sir Geoffrey Howe, who was our Foreign Secretary at the time. He seemed quite unperturbed on the point and repudiated any suggestion that the British government was not fulfilling its obligations under the preamble of the Non-Proliferation Treaty. It was not exactly a noble moment in Britain's post-war history. Here was a chance to achieve the biggest breakthrough ever in genuine world-wide disarmament; but we held back for reasons which were pitiably inadequate. Rajiv could be scornful at such moments and sometimes invoked his mother's favourite poet, Robert Frost, to express his views – as when, during his first speech at the Mansion House in London, before a massed assembly of representatives of the financial companies which had made their fortunes out of his mother's India, he offered his listeners a subtle but pointed comment on relations between the two countries:

Forgive, O Lord, my little jokes on Thee
And I'll forgive Thy great big one on me.

Among other losses when he was murdered by terrorists
on 22 May 1991 were the continued support he would have
given to Mikhail Gorbachev and his continued contempt
for the British policy which favoured Pakistan. If Rajiv
Gandhi had lived he would, I believe, have become an
increasingly powerful voice in the world presenting India's
case. The assassins who killed him, like those who killed
his mother in 1984 and those who killed Mahatma Gandhi
in 1947, were enemies of a truly united India, which could
only survive if it embraced a multitude of different faiths.
The killers were all fanatical nationalists of one breed or
another who saw a powerful India as the enemy they must
fight, literally to the death. And, tragically, the assassina-
tions achieved their objective. The hopes for a larger tolerance seemed wretchedly postponed, and India's own voice
muffled.

One aspect of the nuclear debate was especially well
understood by Mikhail Gorbachev and Rajiv Gandhi.
Although their two countries took different approaches to
the Non-Proliferation Treaty signed in 1970, each knew
how important the treaty was in the attempt to stop the
spread of the techniques and materials needed to make
nuclear weapons. Gorbachev's predecessors had signed the
original document on that account; Rajiv Gandhi's predecessor had refused to do so, since it seemed to decree that
only existing nuclear states would be allowed to continue
to hold such weapons, while all new entrants would be
banned. For India this was an intolerable prospect, not only
on account of Indians' legitimate fears about what Pakistan
was preparing, but because it would mean accepting that

India's situation must remain indefinitely inferior to China's. Such disconcerting consequences as these had been foreseen by some of those who drafted the original treaty; indeed, some of the actual signatories raised similar objections. So, partly to meet this legitimate concern and partly on grounds of sheer common sense or common decency, the preamble to the whole treaty contained the assurance that the nuclear powers themselves were committed to the eventual abolition of nuclear weapons. No date for this happy denouement was inserted, but no doubt was possible about the general intention. And yet, whenever nuclear disarmers in the British House of Commons raised the question of the preamble, as several of us did, we would be brushed aside with the same kind of disdain which Sir Geoffrey Howe had displayed at the Foreign Office. He was much more interested in getting Pakistan's support against the Soviet intruders on their northern border than in enquiring too indelicately into Pakistan's own nuclear developments.

Chapter 4

To the Brink

I would not so purchase
The Empire of Eternity. Hence – hence –
Old Hunter of the earliest brutes! and ye,
Who hunted fellow-creatures as if brutes!
Once bloody mortals – and now bloodier idols,
If your priests lie not! And thou, ghastily Beldame!
Dripping with dusky gore, and trampling on
The carcases of Inde ... away! away! ...

Byron, *Sardanapalus*

Every Indian Prime Minister after Rajiv Gandhi considered whether he should take the next step in testing his country's nuclear capability. They would have been neglectful of their duty if they had not done so, especially in the light of the evidence they constantly received of Chinese or American complicity in helping with Pakistan's programme. Sometimes the political temperature seemed suddenly to rise to boiling point, especially over Kashmir; but it rapidly became apparent that nuclear bombs were no more a solution to that problem than to any other. At other times the tension would subside, the futility of such weapons was exposed, and the Prime Minister concerned might make the quite reputable judgement that he must look afresh at less bellicose ways of proceeding. He might have to resist the pressure of his scientific experts, who wanted action and maybe were even feeding his political opponents with their fears. Although it was not made public at the time, a major 'nuclear' crisis between India and Pakistan did blow up in 1990. 'Much more frightening than Cuba' was the verdict of some American expert observers: an exaggeration, no doubt, but one source of the American interest was that the episode exposed the extent of American intervention on Pakistan's side. However, since some other trends in world affairs were moving in directions which all peace-lovers and most Indians would heartily approve, it would have been sad indeed if India had cut itself off from a genuine participation in these exertions by resorting to military action or military display.

India sustained this open, intelligent approach to the question over the years under various different governments. At the height of one of the controversies on the subject, at the non-aligned summit in Colombia in October 1995, Prime Minister P. V. Narasimha Rao stated the matter thus: 'A handful of nations perpetuated their monopoly over the means of mutually assured destruction by the indefinite extension of the Nuclear Non-Proliferation Treaty. While the aims of these treaties are laudable and we support them wholeheartedly, we must ensure that we do not lose yet another opportunity to obtain a commitment to universal comprehensive nuclear disarmament.'[1] Just after that seemingly reasonable warning, discussions started in the American Congress about the kind of sanctions which might be applied to individual nations which broke the non-proliferation rules. On the face of it, that might seem a reasonable means towards the desired end of stopping the deadly proliferation. But the case was not quite so obvious. John Holum, Director of the United States Arms Control Agency, fielded some awkward questions at a press conference in Washington in February 1996. He was asked to explain why such sanctions had not been applied to China and Pakistan when intelligence agencies had informed the State Department that Beijing had transferred eleven ballistic missiles to Islamabad in violation of the missile technology control regime. The reply was not exactly a repudiation of the charge, but a request that the precise definition of the weapons should be looked at more carefully.

It did seem to the Indians that they were being treated with a special disfavour, and soon similar misapprehensions arose over the negotiations for the signing of a new Comprehensive Test Ban Treaty. As with the NPT provisions, India was strongly in favour of the ultimate objective but strongly opposed to the discrimination which might apply in the meantime. Specifically, India would be signing away its right to repeat the Pokhran test of 1974, abandoning for ever the capacity to become a nuclear power. No Indian administration of the time could have agreed to that proposition, as Arundhati Ghose, India's representative at the conference, insisted. But the Indian objection was never a mere negative one: 'We are of the view that to be meaningful, the treaty should be securely anchored in a global disarmament context and be linked through treaty language to the elimination of all nuclear weapons in a time bound framework.'[2]

The man who put this case more coolly and clearly than anyone else was Inder Kumar Gujral: first as Foreign Minister in 1996–7 and later as Prime Minister in 1997–8. He had taken the opportunity of lecturing primarily on this subject both in the United States and in Britain. No one who heard him could doubt what he was saying or that the views he expressed represented a much wider range of opinion than was directly embodied in the 'United Front' administration of which he had become the leader; nor could there be any doubting the quality of his mind and his conviction that India's case on the CTBT must be heard and in some degree met, if the world at large were to be set on the right course.

Suddenly, quite against his will and on an entirely different issue, he and his government were defeated in parliament and forced into a general election in March 1998. Such disturbances happen in parliamentary democracies. I happened to have an appointment with him in his Delhi office on the evening when the result of the crucial vote was verified. He might have easily cancelled my meeting; but instead he was his usual cool, collected self, ready to talk about the domestic event which had intervened to break up his government, but most concerned as usual with the case India presented to the world. This was the theme to which my conversations with him naturally turned, but interwoven with it were some reflections on the particular topic on which he believed his country's position was most grievously misunderstood, not only by the Americans but often, and to a hardly lesser degree, by British politicians too. He had just had a session with Secretary of State Madeleine Albright in which she had insisted on raising the subject of Kashmir; a matter of months earlier the subject had figured in his discussions with the Foreign Secretary Robin Cook, during the Queen's visit, and again soon afterwards when he had talked with Tony Blair at the Commonwealth Conference in Edinburgh. Always he would present his case with the same good temper and conviction. He had all the details of the latest situation in Kashmir at his fingertips; the administration over which he presided had an especially honourable record in seeking peaceful solutions there. Evidence was growing that its approach was the right one, and that these were the proper ways to sustain the authority of the Kashmir administration and its Chief Minister,

Dr Farook Abdullah. What Prime Minister Gujral and his government offered in this field – the most testing of all for any Indian administration – was a further concerted effort to secure the next stage in a truly *democratic* solution. Was this last best hope to be cast aside, the benefits of all this good work swept away in the imminent election? Somehow none of these disputes or aspirations figured prominently in the campaign debates. It was not the final proof of India's immaturity that the cost of living or the corruption of their politicians competed for attention with these larger choices.

If the exchanges between the parties in the Indian election on nuclear matters were muted, what followed was a full-scale clash between the sub-continental neighbours for which no one was prepared. The trigger, it was said on the Pakistan side, was the BJP manifesto pledge to go ahead with the plan already prepared to 'induct' nuclear weapons. The term might mean anything or nothing; actually to go ahead with the next weapons test, the first with an Indian bomb since 1974, or merely to examine what fresh preparations, diplomatic or otherwise, might be needed before this could be done. George Fernandes, defence minister in the new BJP government, seemed to speak more directly or belligerently than his predecessors, but that might just be his nature. And while he still talked, Pakistan acted, and accompanied its actions with an especially pointed insult to India on the Kashmir issue. The precise sequence of events has some significance.

On 6 April 1998 Pakistan tested its Hatf-V surface-to-surface missile 'Ghauri', a 1500km range weapon system with a claimed payload of 700kg. A Pakistan foreign ministry statement said that a successful flight test had been carried out 'as part of our integrated missile research and development programme'. The test marked 'a step forward' in Pakistan's 'indigenous missile and satellite launch programme'. The testing of Ghauri, which Pakistan saw as an answer to India's short-range Prithvi surface-to-surface missile, set off boisterous celebrations in Pakistan, which had long seemed unable to come up with a credible response to India's missile programme. A banner put up in Islamabad read: *Islam ne har Prithvi ke liye Ghauri paida kiya hai* ('Islam has created a Ghauri for every Prithvi'). Even the choice of name for the Pakistani missile was telling. Ghauri was named after Muhammad of Ghur, the Turkish invader who defeated the Rajput king Prithviraj Chauhan in the second battle of Taarain, near Delhi, in AD 1192. In the mistaken belief that India's missile was named after the Rajput king – in fact, Prithvi (earth) and Agni (fire) are named after the elements – Pakistan had sought to infuse a touch of medieval history into the twentieth-century arms race, hoping maybe that history would repeat itself. In this Islamabad's mindset, it would appear, was not very different from that of Hindu communalist historians in India, who could look back on the rich and varied history of the sub-continent only through a divisive prism that made a fine distinction between 'Muslim' and 'Hindu' elements.

The Kashmir connection at that particular moment was reported by one of India's great journalists: Seema Mustafa, the Delhi correspondent of *The Asian Age*.

To re-paint the present scenario: on April 17, 1998, Pakistan information minister, Mr Mushahid Hussain, accompanied by a high-profile entourage, visited the Muridke camp of the Lashkar-e-Taiba, the military wing of the Markaz Dawawal Irshad. The Lashkar is an outfit, set up in 1987, to train extremists for massacring innocents in Jammu and Kashmir. It is open about this and justifies it in the name of Islam, a cause obviously dear to Mr Hussain's misguided heart. The Lashkar has been holding congregations, distributing pamphlets and generally building up opinion within Pakistan against India for its own distorted sense of justice, manifested by the cold blooded murder of innocent people. Earlier the Pakistan government, behind the *naqab* could be seen shaking its veiled head every time Lashkar and militancy were mentioned. There was no vocal denial, but the shake of the head was taken by the over-eager Indian government to read as a loud 'NO'. But now Pakistan has emerged from behind the *naqab* and the 'No' has become an equally loud 'Yes'. And what better way for Prime Minister Sharif to communicate this but to send his right hand man to the camp? Mr Hussain heard the Markaz chief speak of the liberation of Kashmir and of the liberation of Indian Muslims, and of how visits by politicians like him would help the extremists step up their *jihad* [holy war]. Not to be left behind the minister who should have known better – and there was a time long long ago, when he did seem to know better – endorsed the speeches and went on to speak of *jihad* as the only option. A *maulvi* in political garb. The same night, 29 innocent men, women and children were shot dead by extremists in Jammu and Kashmir. The Lashkar is believed to have taken responsibility for the massacre. There has not been a word from the friendly neighbour about this ghastly murder which was obviously pre-planned. This is not to say that Mr Hussain was the architect, this is to say that the Markaz chief is right in saying that when politicians like him extend both hands and feet in support to such organisations, it gives a major fillip to their activities. Besides, it establishes the direct link between terrorism and the Pakistan government. On 18 April, Pakistan President Rafiq Tarar stepped in, wanting more and more missiles. And not just plain old missiles but missiles named after conquerors. It would have been pathetic had it not been so dangerous. One does not know what Mr Tarar is all about,

but he is the President of Pakistan. And in this position
represents the dignity of the nation he heads. Not just he,
but the entire government of that country seems to be lost
under a bout of amnesia. They are not acting like heads
of state but more like the audience watching a C-grade
Bollywood *masala* film replete with catcalls and loud wolf
whistles. If in the process some die, and others are killed,
it is not the responsibility of the audience.[3]

Some supposedly mature military judgements added to the
fury. Pakistani experts were especially angered by the Indian
slur that their Ghauri was a foreign import.

Denial of the credibility of Ghauri is a mechanism to bolster
bruised ego. If it is that fictional, why so much of fuss about
the issue? Surely there are some grey areas in Ghauri, as in
all such inventions, but our scientists are capable of rec-
tifying them and improve upon its efficiency. To attribute
it as a gift of the Chinese or Koreans, is an infantile way of
facing the reality. Rocketry is not a new art to Muslims. In
his book, *The Sun of Islam*, Dr Hunke writes: 'While we are
amazed by breathtaking progress of modern rocket technology, it seldom occurs to us to whom we owe this invention.
We Westerners do not like to think about its origin. An
engineer from Damascus and his sons, Abu Bakr, Ibrahim
and Mohammad constructed seven large rocket machines,
which Kublay Khan used to break China's last resistance.'[4]

The Prankote massacre was the most violent communal
killing to have taken place in Jammu and Kashmir for ten
years; and the method of the killing was even worse than
the original report.

Although there had been several major communal killings
in the 1990s, the brutality of Prankote was almost unprecedented. The terrorists of the Lashkar-e-Toiba [The Army

of the Pious] carried out the act. Not a single shot was fired. Instead, the victims had their throats slit. In several cases they were decapitated but their limbs were sawed off. Others were burnt alive; four bodies were discovered in the debris of one of the four homes that were burnt by the terrorists. Nine of the dead were children. Contrary to claims put out by some newspapers, on the basis of an inaccurate Agence France Presse report from Jammu, the killing was not the outcome of local Hindus refusing to convert to Islam. Rather, the objectives of the massacre were rooted in politics and could have serious long-term implications for India–Pakistan relations. News of the massacre reached the surrounding villages rather late. Homes in the hills are separated by considerable distances, and since no shots were fired, many people knew nothing about the incident immediately. Vidya Devi and her children remained near the stream, refusing to emerge. Another woman, Bittoo Devi, had managed to hide in the fields behind her father Shobha Ram's house along with her sisters, Balo Devi and Anjoy Devi. She returned to the house before dawn to see if there were any survivors, but was caught by the terrorists and set on fire. The children, who were too scared to follow their sister, survived. Residents of Narkote village, across the stream from Prankote, saw the flames from Shobha Ram's house, but did not act, from fear or incomprehension. 'Early in the morning Bittoo staggered into my house,' recalls Baldev Singh, a resident of Narkote village, 'charred like a log. She kept asking us for clothes to cover her body, which we gave her. She died minutes later, after which we, although scared for our lives, set out to see what had happened.'[5]

All these events, however horrific in themselves and in their effect on neighbouring states, might be dismissed as post-election skirmishes. On Monday 11 May the new Indian government of Atal Behari Vajpayee carried out three nuclear tests at the Pokhran range where the original Indian tests had been staged in 1974. Two days later, two more tests were carried through at the same place. The second performance in one sense was even more startling than the first, since the first round seemed to provoke world-wide protest, especially in the United States from President Clinton. He seemed aggrieved, as if the new Indian premier had offered him some personal affront. Maybe his annoyance was increased by the fact that his own secret service, supposedly the best in the world, had not warned him precisely when the tests were to take place. Since, as he later insisted, he regarded the matter as one of global significance, he should have been better informed on the politics involved, let alone the espionage.

Whatever the rights and wrongs of the Indian decision – and, of course, that great argument still proceeds – it is quite unfair to all the Indian parties involved to suggest that India had been engaged in some grand deception of the international community. The exact opposite was the case. Indian leaders had refused to sign the CTBT – and had indeed invited much annoyance from President Clinton on this account – because they knew that this would forbid them from ever acquiring nuclear weapons. Whatever else they did, they had to keep that option open; otherwise they would play into the hands of their own domestic breed of raging nationalists. If the Indians were the unconscionable deceivers depicted by the Americans, they could have signed the treaty and still proceeded to make the bombs; a deception not unknown in the previous history of nuclear development. The scruple shown by previous Indian governments should have been sufficient on its own to induce a more measured response in Washington. Instead, the outbursts of presidential rage there merely intensified the expression of nationalist pride which swept across India and seemed for a while to banish every other sentiment or consideration. Some of these triumphalist outbursts were ugly in the extreme. The Rashtriya Swayamsevak Sangh (RSS) – the Hindu secret organization widely believed to be the power behind the BJP – saw the explosions as a fresh symbol of their deep-seated racist gospel. However, these were by no means the only elements who saw reason to rejoice. The Indian scientists concerned had proved their capacity. In Indira Gandhi's day they had thought that the devices would be developed only for peaceful purposes. Now that constriction was lifted, and a response offered to the Ghauri threat from Pakistan still drumming in their ears.

President Clinton's rhetoric seemed to be designed for a different planet. Just before the explosions, his special emissary had been taken to the Pakistan camps where the terrorists were trained for their ruthless, persistent incursions into Kashmir. Evidence of the last atrocity was plain to see – the bodies of the victims massacred at Prankote, mostly pious Hindus, were still lying on the ground. It was not altogether surprising, albeit quite illogical, when Kashmir's Chief Minister Farook Abdullah welcomed the tests and the renewed proof they seemed to give of Indian determination. He would have to discover later, like others before him, that nuclear bombs are no use for such beneficent purposes. But his outburst offered a striking example of how tense the political situation had become, and how spectacular, if senseless, was the relief which the tests seemed to offer. At almost exactly the same moment the Dalai Lama of Tibet, not normally a belligerent figure but one who had suffered and seen his country suffer from Chinese tyranny, ventured the same kind of judgement as Farook about the benefits which might be felt across his part of Asia from such a shift in the military balance.

The Indian response, then, was something more than the insensate nationalist outburst hailed by the RSS. It was partly an expression of a pent-up protest against India's supposed friends in the Western world – President Clinton foremost among them – who had never troubled to discover the real problems of sustaining a modern democracy. They even dared to use the word 'hegemony'. That was what India was alleged to be seeking with its three tests, inviting on its head every kind of punishment. We need not be so surprised that the nuclear hegemony of the United States is hated more in India than anywhere else.

Such almighty power has indeed been given specific legal form, inscribed into law framed according to their sacred American Constitution. Clinton cited such laws to prove that he must act as he did. His administration and its predecessor had been involved in quarrels over the supply of aircraft to Pakistan which might conceivably be used to carry nuclear cargoes. At the time of a previous dispute with India it was thought this objection might be waived, however much such a course offended American law. But when India carried out its tests, the application of sanctions of unspecified severity had, apparently, to be automatic. This was one reason why Clinton could not stop to consider, even with the friendliest powers such as Britain, whether this was indeed the best way to secure the common objective of a genuine world-wide ban on the distribution of nuclear materials. In fact, the American policy was one designed to preserve the American hegemony. As the controversy intensified, this awkward fact was pointed out by former President Carter – not the first American President, as we have previously noted, to acquire a fresh wisdom after he had left the White House.

We may permit ourselves another glance at the choice which the Indians made themselves. Previous Indian Prime Ministers had known that they had the scientific knowledge and apparatus to undertake such tests but still refrained from doing so. The first was Indira Gandhi in the 1970s; there is no reason to question her own claim that she was overwhelmingly convinced that the development would be used only for peaceful purposes. From Pakistan, President Bhutto made the charge that India had initiated a sinister nuclear plot; the record speaks differently. Rajiv Gandhi, in the 1980s, was both concerned by developments in Pakistan's own nuclear programme and fully aware that Pakistan had powerful nuclear allies. But he helped to devise the best solution of all: the world-wide application of the Delhi Declaration of 1986. What he would have done if he had won the election of 1991 instead of being assassinated, we can only guess. He certainly could not have allowed Pakistan to move ahead in this most fateful competition – as he had explained to me – but he still would have had a further chance of framing another genuine international initiative with his friend Gorbachev. Two other Indian Prime Ministers considered the nuclear option and reached somewhat different conclusions. Prime Minister Narasimha Rao came near to giving the order but was apparently dissuaded in the end by interventions from Washington. Prime Minister Gujral brought to bear on the choice a sophisticated training in foreign affairs and a deep sense of responsibility. He was the living proof that India had *not* engaged in the alleged great deception. As Prime Minister, he had even undertaken a special visit to the United States to ensure that India's apprehensions about the CTBT were properly understood. Maybe his approach was too subtle for some to appreciate. He thought that the value of India's bomb was greater before it was tested: who could forecast exactly what would be the fallout, diplomatic, economic and the rest, once the tests had actually taken place? He did not hold back from giving the final order through any kind of weakness or fear. He did prescribe what he considered an intelligent policy for seeking better relations with India's neighbours, including Pakistan. The rupture in that relationship came entirely from Pakistan, and he did his best to warn the Americans among others how dangerous for the whole sub-continent were the tactics which Pakistan was pursuing and raising to a new pitch of fervour in Kashmir.

Prime Minister Atal Behari Vajpayee (Atom Bomb Vajpayee, as he was soon nicknamed) was not at all the fire-eating military leader which his action seemed to imply and which his BJP followers dearly wished him to become. The paradox of his position was that his personality contrasted sharply with the raucous, rampaging new nationalism which his party sought to represent. How these wild forces had grown so prodigiously in recent times was something of a mystery. The rise of the BJP may have owed more to the combined follies and crimes of their opponents than to any other single factor, but it owed something too to the parliamentary skills of their leader, the assurance he seemed to give that his India was still the India which had come to nationhood in the 1940s and had its own proper part to play in the larger world. He had had many of his own quarrels with previous Indian governments, and different appreciations as was now revealed, on the question of the nuclear tests. On every previous occasion when he had been in office, he claimed to have considered the possibility of giving the order to go ahead; when he actually gave it and the deed was done, the immediate patriotic response went far beyond anything anyone could have foretold. He became overnight a much more powerful figure than he had ever been before. What he did not say at the time – his most grievous failure – was that the testing of the bombs was, for India and for the world at large, a bad second best. What was needed was a full-scale international regime which would make such explosions unnecessary. Every previous Indian Prime Minister had spoken in those terms, establishing the consistent theme which gave India its truest distinction.

Fair-minded observers of the scene, especially those in foreign capitals accustomed to the language of international debate, might deplore the new policy in such terms as these; but something sharper still, produced on Indian soil, was needed to define both the domestic turmoil and the international perspective. Seema Mustafa filled the role pre-eminently well on both counts. She had already reported in *The Asian Age*, more observantly than any of her colleagues on other newspapers, the fateful intrusions which Pakistan was making across the Kashmir border. She was at the Delhi press conference when the Prime Minister made his statement about the tests of 11 May. She reported the matter thus in her newspaper on 16 May.

India has gone nuclear. It is in the big league now knocking at the doors of the exclusive nuclear club for admission. There is a national consensus, or so one is told, of a deep sense of satisfaction and pride that now we have arrived. We have told the world where it stands, where we are, and what we can do. We have announced through a series of five nuclear explosions that we have finally developed the muscles that the world recognises and we cannot be fooled around with. For now we are equal partners in the boxing ring and can land a punch with equal ferocity. Or at least that is what we are being fed by our information managers, be they of the foreign office variety or the more plebian Press Information Bureau.

The first inkling that something was on came when we, ordinary scribes, were informed that the Prime Minister had scheduled a quick press conference. At his residence – the stars were obviously right for he had shifted exactly on the day the explosions were conducted – the staff was rushing to make the arrangements for the press conference. There was major domo Pramod Mahajan in freshly starched kurta-pajama overseeing the arrangements, particularly from the eye of the television camera. There was Press Information officer, S. Narendra following instructions and placing flower pots according to Mahajan's aesthetic sense. Narendra, in fact, became very busy removing pots with few flowers and bringing in the ones with more blossoms. Important work, indeed, judging from the attention it got from the Prime Minister's senior staff members.

Then came the Indian flag and it was draped over a small mast. Instead of flying in the air the flag, probably against all prescribed protocol, fell over the mast as backdrop for the Prime Minister. The doors finally opened and the Prime Minister came out to break the stunning news which was designed to arouse an unquestioning brand of nationalism that would consolidate the BJP and override all criticism, not just about the blasts but against the party and its government.

It has done just that, setting into motion an agenda which is aimed at appeasing the hardliners of the RSS and the BJP and arousing the passion of 'nationalism' in the middle class and the nuclear elite which have closed its ears to all words of caution. To express a doubt about the political wisdom of this decision is to risk being dubbed an anti-national and if you carry a Muslim name, as this columnist does, it will probably be sufficient to throw you across the border on to the 'other' side.

The background was well prepared. The RSS handled its constituency through its mouthpieces using Pakistan's missile, Ghauri, to hit out at China and conjure up images of Sino-Pakistan collusion. Defence minister George Fernandes was the missile hurled at the country at large and he went on a hectic tour programme attacking China in every breath. He used the classic RSS system of distortion and falsehoods, speaking of old disputes as if he had fresh information, and vaguely hinting about the construction of helipads in Indian territory by the Chinese which did not exist. The foreign office was reined in by Prime Minister Vajpayee and except for one statement Fernandes remained unchecked. Judging from the reaction now, he had a major impact in rekindling all the old suspicions and fears about China.

What he has not said and the BJP government has not explained, and nor will it explain, is what was the fresh provocation. Prime Minister Vajpayee has written to the US President claiming that the Chinese threat was a major reason behind the nuclear explosions and India's sudden desire to be recognised as a nuclear weapon state. In fact from all indications Sino-Indian relations were improving. There was not a word of hostility from the Chinese to justify the fear psychosis set into motion by the defence minister and his government. But a large section of the population lapped it all up, as his master planners knew they would.

The plan is clear: recognise India as a nuclear weapon state and we will sign the CTBT. Much will depend on the attitude of the big five but the possibility of recognition is very high. Perhaps it was agreed upon earlier with the US as some like to maintain, and perhaps it was not. That has become immaterial, as now India is obviously carving out a new future for itself on the plea that this will spell security in an increasingly threatening global scenario.

Based on this is the real BJP agenda. The bomb is to

consolidate itself at home. A tottering government, torn apart by pressures from the allies; a vacillating Prime Minister unable to act; a Hindutva agenda pushing into the backwaters through sheer political compulsions; an economic programme torn between the swadeshi lobby and the so-called pragmatists; rising criticism from the BJP constituency . . . these and more pressures could be eased with one fell stroke. The bomb.

The government has, through this one action, acquired the sanction based on the so-called national consensus to act for the nation. It has now the legitimacy to set into motion the agenda based on the RSS/BJP brand of nationalism, inherent in which is intolerance and discrimination. Dissent at this stage will not be tolerated, not just by the hardliners but even by the middle class and the nuclear elite which have this very unquestioning and very outdated attitude about national interests. For instance, the nuclear option is in the national interest and any argument to the contrary arouses anger and condemnation.

There were two choices before India: to build peace or to build a bomb. Congress Prime Minister in 1996, Narasimha Rao, flirted with the bomb but backed out the minute the Americans got to know about it and exerted pressure. He had taken it up for some of the same reasons as Vajpayee. His popularity was on the wane, the economy was sagging, unrest was growing, disillusionment was at its peak and the bomb would have put all this into the background – at least for some time – and given a resounding national pat on the back to Rao.

Former Prime Minister Inder Kumar Gujral was perhaps correct in telling Vajpayee that the file had been on every Prime Minister's table at least for some time. Gujral did not use the option for two basic reasons. One, he was trying to broker peace and did not believe in war. Two, the United Front constituency did not need to be fed with the bomb. The poor in the villages which were essentially

the electorate that had brought most of the Front constitu-
ents into power at one time, could not have been consoli-
dated with the bomb. Drinking water would be, and it still
is, for that matter, a more potent weapon for rallying this
electorate. India is divided between a small minority that is
articulate and influences opinion and the sizeable majority
that is poor, oppressed and does not have a voice. When the
political powers talk of a national consensus, the reference is
to the articulate minority which is well fed, educated, has
the money to shop abroad, believes in the bomb and con-
veniently forgets the toiling millions living in utter poverty
in the villages and slums of India.

These millions live without drinking water, fall prey to
every disease, are the targets of natural calamities, have no
education, do not get one square meal a day, and their
children have no future. But to tend to them would not
have the dramatic results of the nuclear kind. Drinking
water and food in every single village would really make
India strong, but these kind of schemes call for planning,
dedication and sacrifice; three qualities that our political
leaders, of any colour, have not been known for.

Today India has gone against the emerging world consensus for disarmament and nuclear non-proliferation. Of
course, this is being interpreted here as a sign of strength,
a 'we will do what we want' syndrome. But in doing what
we want, are we strengthening India in the long run or
weakening it? This is the question that needs to be answered
in full honesty and detail. The big talk after the event has
also not helped in formulating a mature response to the
hostile world opinion that is pouring in. The question is
not of withstanding sanctions, but of withstanding political
isolation and being reduced to a very small player in the
world arena.

This is not to support the hypocrisy of the nuclear
nations, but to condemn it. That nuclear bombs are just for
some nations who are supposedly more civilised to play with

these. The same bombs become explosive and dangerous in the hands of the brown skins. Sic. But this kind of racism cannot be fought by accepting the racists' yardstick for power. And the condemnation has little meaning when India herself is clamouring to join the club. The opposition to the Comprehensive Test Ban Treaty on principled grounds, the opposition to the right of some nations to create two categories, the country's claim to speak for the non-nuclear nations of the world – all this has come to an end with the bomb. Membership is clearly a sign of prowess and power for the same country that was earlier so sure that it did not want or need this particular certificate. The BJP manifesto and agenda is committed to nuclearisation. The government says that it will now fight to remove the discriminatory clauses from the CTBT and the NPT. There is talk and there is reality. The reality might not be so easy, for the global dynamics that have been unleashed by the explosions might just step outside India's control. Unfortunately, the lumpen elements have been unleashed to project the bomb in all its jingoistic proportions. There has been no attempt by the government and the party to make its cadre exorcise anarchy, with the sobriety that should have been associated with the event having been discarded for ultra-nationalist posturing.

Where will India go from here? What does it want? What is the world view? What now? Domestically, in a different time from today, Indira Gandhi was unable to consolidate her constituency with the bomb. Within 10 months after the first nuclear test and the big fanfare, she had to impose Emergency. Internationally, India has lost her friends, old and new, and will have to build relations from scratch. Being in the nuclear club will not earn her the trust and respect of all those countries who have chosen to stay out of it, not because they do not have the where-withal to join but because they have taken a conscious decision not to join. Domestic memory is short but international memory is long. India might or might not be accepted into the nuclear club but the international community will ensure that she pays the price. The price is fine so long as it is worth it. Is it? That is a question that has not been answered. And if it is not, it will not be Vajpayee but the people of India who will be made to deliver. For in the final analysis, it is not the nuclear elite but the toiling masses who pay for bad political decisions with their sweat and blood.[6]

Such is the proper level on which the debate should be conducted. Many recent visitors to India have noted how high is the standard of writing sustained in the Indian press: not merely in New Delhi, with such journals as *The Hindustani Times* and *The Times of India*, but also in *The Hindu* and *Frontline* in Madras and now in *The Asian Age* itself, covering several waterfronts. If this was a British bequest along with the language, it is certainly an inheritance which has helped at moments of crisis to protect India's freedom, its most precious democracy. Even so, there are not so very many who dare to write, or can write, like Seema Mustafa – any more than there were once many to rival James Cameron.

India's reputation in the world was something worth having. The weakest part of the new Prime Minister's method of operation was his apparent readiness to cast aside this huge international asset. Leaders of nations who choose to play the game of realpolitik should show some recognition of the rules and the risks. American practice in that very theatre of operations where Indian interests so justly clamoured for recognition had often been exercised in a most injurious manner. Once upon a time communist China had been the great enemy against whom all good peoples, including India, must be rallied. Then, for a few decades,

China was transformed into a valued opponent of the Soviet Union; so China must be granted accommodations of its own, which included tolerance of its entry into the nuclear club and, even more exasperating from India's point of view, an American connivance with Chinese backing for Pakistan, including even the supply of some materials for the manufacture of nuclear weapons. All through the 1980s the United States was more interested in securing Pakistan's support against the Soviet Union's activities in Afghanistan than in the particular military supplies which Pakistan might wish to acquire for its own use. Ever since 1962, when hostilities between the two countries had ceased along that lengthy frontier, China had continued to hold territory which India believed was properly its own. Sometimes the normal asperities between the two countries would soften, only to be renewed in all their ferocity overnight, for quite extraneous reasons. While the Soviet Union still existed, India had an ally which could encourage better manners in Beijing. But when that prop was removed, no one could guess exactly what developments might follow. China had been a nuclear power since the early 1960s; it had conducted its most recent round of tests in 1996. Afterwards, having timed them to suit its own convenience, China, like some other powers, was ready to sign the CTBT, with its prohibition on the supply to other countries of materials for making nuclear weapons. With communist China, whatever its nuclear capacity, it seemed to be a settled part of American policy to exercise an astonishing degree of patience. With India, a quite different set of rules, regulations and moral judgements were brought into play.

Ironically, this was the most legitimate reason for the Indian action of May 1998. In a world ruled by force, they must equip themselves with adequate weapons. The arguments of their scientists and military advisers sounded irrefutable; and so, in the old military sense, they were. What they left out of the account was the futility of the weapons themselves. They could not be used to avenge the Prankote massacre, to defend Kashmir from the terrorists or even to play an effective role in the kind of war Pakistan had launched against India on previous occasions. As the competition had developed over the past two decades, each now had the capacity to exterminate all the main cities of the other. They may even have acquired that ultimate sophistication of the nuclear armouries – the ability to do it by accident.

When India carried out its tests, Pakistan immediately replied that it would soon do the same. The Prime Minister, Nawaz Sharif, delivered the retort at once: the question was not whether but when. Expressions of anti-Indian feeling on the streets of Islamabad and most other cities in Pakistan were ferocious and sustained. A few voices were raised suggesting that Sharif had neither the necessary preparations in place nor the stomach for effective retaliation. If it had been so, he would have been swiftly overthrown: there are ample precedents in Pakistan's short history for the summary removal of a civilian leader who failed to execute orders from the military. But Sharif was as good as, or even better than, his word. He resisted a whole series of frantic appeals not to go ahead, including a lengthy and passionate telephone call from President Clinton. A series of tests was carried out in the Chaghi fields in Baluchistan, which had long been prepared for the purpose.

Just before Sharif gave the order deemed essential to protect Pakistan's independence, an extraordinary scare penetrated official circles in Islamabad. The rumour was that an Israeli aeroplane could and would inflict a pre-emptive strike on those Chaghi fields where the tests were scheduled to take place. Israel was no friend of India; however, it was even more an enemy of Pakistan, which it suspected of being ready to use its nuclear facilities to assist other Islamic states, most worryingly Iran, to take another step along the same perilous course. Once before in nuclear history Israel had taken such pre-emptive action, with its monstrously illegal but highly successful attack against Iraq in 1981. An unidentified F-16 flying over the Chaghi Hills in the morning of 25 May, before the test operations started, was sufficient to provoke enquiries or protests via Washington to Tel Aviv. Both swiftly repudiated the accusation that they were engaged in any activity so scandalous. However, a few days later a different explanation was offered: 'The surveillance could well be the result of Tel Aviv's dissatisfaction with the quality of American intelligence on Pakistan's nuclear activities and failure of the CIA to have provided adequate forewarning of India's nuclear tests.'[7] With all such alarms suddenly subdued, Pakistan went ahead with its own tests, more numerous than India's if not quite so powerful, yet demonstrating a capability sufficient, if ever used in earnest, to emulate the horror of Hiroshima. The scale of the rejoicing in Islamabad, Lahore and every other Pakistani city seemed to outdo anything in New Delhi. Islam's bomb defied the world – India, America, Israel. It might well have been that those Israeli pilots could have received different instructions, and if they had, the devastation spread across Baluchistan would undoubtedly have been attributed to India's aggression. Thanks to the nature of nuclear weapons, such are the slender threads on which may hang the unleashing of a new holocaust.

Some of the most astute observers of the crisis in New Delhi wondered whether Nawaz Sharif would have the wit and the courage to adopt the Israel Syndrome. President Clinton was obviously amazed that he refused to do so. M. J. Akbar offered his classic definition of the Israel Syndrome in the 1 June issue of his newspaper, *The Asian Age*. Any American liberals or democrats of whatever brand or breed still wondering why their country no longer commands the kind of allegiance it commanded in the days of Roosevelt or Eisenhower may usefully study the conduct of their leader in this whole episode. He spoke as if he were entitled to speak for the international community on the supreme matters of life and death – and, considering only the nature of the weapons, so he was; but a quite different application of the law had been applied to Israel, not merely in that moment of crisis, but for years.

Clinton, wrote Akbar in that article,

> was genuinely surprised therefore when Pakistan preferred a public bomb to the Israel Syndrome. The Israel Syndrome should not need too much explanation; it is a matter of having your bomb and eating it too. Only the truly stupid may think that Israel does not have a nuclear weapons capability. Israel has not mortgaged its security to America; it has its own bomb as the answer to the Arab threat of annihilation. But by the simple ruse of denying this fact, Israel gets the best of both worlds: the financial support and technology it needs from America, and the confidence it needs at home. This is a game played by all the political parties of Israel as well as its friends across the world. Israel never felt the compulsion to test its capabilities and either invite hostility or give countries like Iraq and Iran formal reason for a public demonstration of their own nuclear weapons programme. Rather than advertise its bomb, Israel punishes any citizen claiming knowledge of its secret. Only its enemies need to know about deterrence, not its friends. If it had not been for the clamour on the city streets, Sharif

could have made that response. The real horror scenario
for India was the possibility that Pakistan would opt for
subterfuge instead of public confrontation. Pakistan has had
good practice these last fifty years at the art of looking
pained in public; all it needed to do was dab a few tears. The
United States had already initiated the process of supplying
Pakistan with all the conventional arms that it needed, and
Islamabad could have had World Bank funding for them if
it so desired.[8]

Paradoxically, the bomb, once tested, tended to lose
rather than gain in diplomatic leverage. How much influence Sharif had cast away in those frenzied days it is impossible to estimate. India, too, had in some sense committed
the same gigantic error. Akbar noted the point with his
usual acumen. Sharif might have done 'what we were doing
under eight Prime Ministers since 1974: creating a private
capability while the world agreed to look the other way.'[9]
If Sharif had been able to continue such restraint, how much
more powerful his position would have been. If India's ninth
Prime Minister had been able to sustain that position, how
much more powerful India's position would have been.
Number Eight on the list, Prime Minister Gujral, argued
the case for continued restraint as authoritatively and per-
sistently as any of his predecessors; and when his successor,
Prime Minister Vajpayee, made the fateful change in policy
he persisted in his opposition to it, arguing that there was
no change in the international scene to warrant the major
change of policy. Prime Minister Gujral, as noted earlier,
was deeply critical of US policy towards India. He argued
as strongly as anyone else that both the Non-Proliferation
Treaty and the Comprehensive Test Ban Treaty were
in their existing forms grossly unfair to countries like
India, but also that they could still be transformed into

instruments for the abolition of all nuclear arsenals. When he made the accusation that he knew of no new threat, no change in the international situation to warrant Vajpayee's change in policy, he was accused of failing to understand the new pressures from Pakistan or China and over Kashmir. But there was no basis for such a deduction; he was well aware of all these complications and would present them to other participants in the international debate, from Secretary of State Albright to Prime Minister Blair. The defeat of his government in the March 1998 election had nothing whatever to do with international policy; it was a tragedy for India, and maybe the world. The Gujral doctrine conformed much more closely to the kind of world which independent India had hitherto sought to establish than the policy adopted by his successor.

How severe is the damage wrought by this change? Is it irreparable? Was the new India thereby set on a course which will forbid any chance of democratic recovery, condemned never to escape from an ever-darkening tunnel of insensate nationalism, a ferocious and futile reflection of what was happening in Pakistan? For a while, little distinction could be drawn between the raucous cries for fresh signs of belligerence in Islamabad and in New Delhi. But then something else happened: a miracle almost, if a perverse one. Overnight, Pakistan became a police state. The parliament was called for the purpose of suspending all civil rights and imposing a complete state of emergency. But India remained a democracy; and the manner in which India used its democratic institutions changed the immediate prospect and maybe some longer perspectives too.

Akbar described the parliamentary scene in memorable, generous terms. His report was significant chiefly for his understanding of how brave it was for the opposition to withstand the jingoistic mood in the streets outside, but he also found time for a perceptive glance at the Prime Minister's role. The Indian parliament itself had not often played such a distinguished part. This time it rose to the height of the great argument.

The level of the debate on the nuclear explosions was a fine example of tremendous strength and maturity that India has acquired over fifty years. The debate in Parliament was a superb assault on jingoism and helped bury the excesses that had surrounded the nuclear tests. Politicians have an inherent tendency to play safe in a democracy on issues with strong patriotic overtones, for their future is determined by votes. The 'judicious' thing to do for all the Opposition parties would have been to congratulate the government, duck, and hope that Jayalalitha would return to the headlines as soon as possible. Instead, all the parties in the Opposition, without exception, risked the anger of jingoists and questioned and probed the government's nuclear weapons policy. They asked whether the implications had been thought through; they demanded to know whether the government understood the finances involved in a weapons race; they challenged the treasury benches to suggest that patriotism was the BJP's personal monopoly; they questioned the government's motives. Chidambaram made a particularly fine speech, while Somnath Chatterjee was armed with his usual skilful hammer and Natwar Singh surprised the House with the force of his reasoning; and P. A. Sangmar, who is emerging as the surprise orator of this House, snubbed the bomb lobby with conviction and courage. Rarely has defence minister George Fernandes been so defensive; and certainly he was not in the House when a dismissive Somnath Chatterjee suggested to the Prime Minister that the sooner he got rid of his defence minister, the better it would be even for the BJP. And the Prime Minister, when he concluded the debate, reflected the sentiment of the whole House; he spoke of good sense and reassurance and peace built on strength. Mr Atal Behari Vajpayee is always at his best when he is being himself rather than a leader of the BJP. But partisan matters aside, this was democracy at its very best. How often has reason stood up to challenge excess and survived to tell the tale? This was dissent in a nation confident about itself; and the message that went out not only to India but to the world was that India could be trusted with a responsible place in its affairs.[10]

Soon after these tense Indian debates, where at least there was much to be said on both sides of the question, real decision-making or some supposed approach to it was transferred to various international bodies where India's case was either scarcely heard at all or roughly pushed aside. The joint communiqué issued by the five nuclear powers meeting in Geneva on 5 June declared that 'they will actively encourage India and Pakistan to find mutually acceptable solutions through direct dialogue which addressed the root cause of the tension, including Kashmir'. No mention was made in the communiqué of India's claim that the cause of the troubles in Kashmir was Pakistan-sponsored terrorism across the border, or of the assurances given by India about a moratorium on future tests, or of India's interest in larger, longer-term questions. Secretary of State Albright stonewalled questions on all these topics. It looked, however, as if she had gained a diplomatic victory on the sore subject of Kashmir. All previous Indian governments – especially, it might be said, the Indian government headed by Prime Minister Gujral – had refused to accept that this was an international problem to be settled by outside mediation. Under Gujral's administration, considerable progress had been made in restoring the authority of the democratically elected administration in Kashmir. He had himself told Madeleine Albright, with his customary politeness, that the proposed American intervention could only upset the apple-cart, with incalculable consequences for the people of Kashmir themselves. And this warning had been issued before the massacre of Prankote. For a while it seemed as if a first casualty of the Indian tests was the best policy for Kashmir supported by all the Indian parties.

Soon the responsibility for the indiscriminate denunciation of India and Pakistan was transferred from the five-power nuclear club to the United Nations Security Council in New York, and that body too accepted without demur this fresh application of the American hegemony. Many peace campaigners all over the world had looked for the day when India would take its rightful place on the Security Council as one of the surest safeguards that the goal of world-wide disarmament would never be abandoned. If the new India had impaired its claim to that role, it was a tragedy which might extend far beyond her shores. The new United States seemed determined to see the Security Council transformed into its obedient instrument, most especially if nuclear matters were involved. The new Russia, the new China, the new France, even the new Britain concurred with varying degrees of docility. Each might have its own particular reasons, not necessarily discreditable, for seeking American friendship or favours. But, translated into the terms of the nuclear arms race, that Security Council resolution would mean not a single reduction in their own five nuclear arsenals, nor even the application of some blessed swift surveillance at those still explosive, disease-threatened fields at Pokhran or Chaghi. There are plenty of trained experts available for the work; but they must have equal access to all sites, with no Israel Syndrome, or British and American ones for that matter, inviting exceptions to the rule. Anyone who objects to this should be given a copy of H. G. Wells's classic *The World Set Free* and instructed to learn how the first Security Council did its job properly, without any discrimination whatever against late developers or lesser breeds. Most curiously, the hero who played the chief part in saving us in Wells's novel was a Russian; and he bore a striking resemblance to the Mikhail Gorbachev many of us saw in action.

*

While the Security Council was passing its resolution and both India and Pakistan were expressing their opposition to it, a somewhat different response was forthcoming from the meeting of the ruling National Conference – the party coalition which supported the Kashmir administration – in Srinagar on 8 June. This resolution was in no sense dictated by the new government in New Delhi; indeed, it contained some direct criticisms of George Fernandes' utterances about relations with China, which were felt to be especially ill-advised. The Conference was much more concerned by the direct threat from Pakistan. Moreover, in the eyes of those present, the worst offence had been committed elsewhere:

> Having failed in all their tricks in the past, the interested imperialist expansionist forces and self-elected cops of the world have set themselves the game to destabilise our country, and, in this regard, not only by threats directly issued, but indirectly too by seeking unabashed interference in India's national affairs which are twin instruments tried to be used today . . . Opposition was promised to all nefarious plans to tamper with the territorial integrity of the state, as an integral part of the Union of India . . . No matter who

ruled the country, Kashmir state has to have its glorious cherished autonomous position in the states of the Union as envisaged by decisions taken as far back as in 1947 or 1952.[11]

Most of the language in this resolution was doubtless framed by Dr Farook Abdullah, and he would claim that he was merely sustaining the best traditions of his famous father, the Sheikh who had played such an honourable part in founding the state. But the precise terms of the resolution were the nearest Kashmir as a whole could come to a *democratic* expression of the road it wished to travel in the future. Paradoxically, but none the less surely, the election in Kashmir had proved that much. Partly because of the threats coming from across the Pakistan border, partly because of the coldest weather of the century, the poll there had had to be put off for a week, and the results were by no means a simple victory for Chief Minister Farook or the National Conference whose policies he had sought to implement – much less so for the BJP victors in other parts of India, whose policies threatening the existing status of Kashmir were one of the causes of the trouble. For all the cross-voting that occurred, and irrespective of the frustrations of individual candidates, Kashmir had used its vote to keep open that democratic path to a decent future.

Between 13 May, the day of the most recent tests at Pokhran, and the time of writing some five months later, Indians in their thousands or maybe tens of thousands – since that's their normal way of operating – have mounted the most powerful, well-informed campaign against nuclear weapons anywhere in the world since the demonstrations of the 1950s or the 1980s. Some expert American or British observers had their own reasons for disregarding or deprecating the scale of those protests; but to do so was the kind of foolish error which full-time practising politicians often make in these circumstances. This time they should have known better, especially since some propagandist of genius had the idea of telling the world at large what was happening in India's protest movement. For several weeks on end, before the authorities could cut it down, a huge balloon the size of the Taj Mahal itself was attached to that most famous monument proclaiming the doctrine of peace for which modern India had always stood. And this declaration was backed with a most formidable array of arguments.

India, as we sometimes forget, is a good deal closer to Japan than we are, and the persistent horrors of Hiroshima and Nagasaki are much more sympathetically commemorated there. For the Indians, as for the Japanese, these were unconscionable crimes for which there had never been a breath of apology by the perpetrators, the Americans or their British allies. One of the most moving events in the aftermath of the Indian tests was the trip by a group of Japanese visitors to the Pokhran fields, where the talk was not of India's scientific triumphs but of the real meaning of the radioactive poison.

In those far-off times just after Hiroshima and Nagasaki, or even ten years later when the Americans conducted their tests at Bikini, a huge propaganda effort had been devoted to playing down the threat to future generations. No doubt the Indian government which gave the order for the 1998 tests would have eagerly availed itself of similar facilities for distortion or suppression; but in democratic India no such protection for the government in Delhi, whatever its complexion, is available. The truth about the Japanese experience is better understood in India. Indeed, since May

1998 a number of Indian writers have been prompted to look afresh at the Hiroshima episode and its aftermath. Sukumar Muralidharan reported in the *Frontline* issue of 14 August, the nearest to the anniversary:

> But that day [Hiroshima Day] things seemed different: 'It was dark, as if the sun had disappeared in the thick black air and swirling wind. My mother had taught me to "live" if an air raid came – to flee fire, to seek the river. But now, there seemed to be no alternative to death as the earth heaved.' 'No alternative to death' – that is the fundamental feature of the nuclear weapon. All rules of engagement in warfare allow some room to escape. Not merely today, but perhaps in varying measures all through history, humanitarian norms have accorded the non-combatant population a degree of protection from the violence and brutality of warfare. Nuclear weapons compel humanity to unlearn all that it has imbibed in the crucible of conflict over the centuries. The ultimate instrument of terror leaves no avenues open. And there is nothing else known that kindles primordial horrors, awakens the irrational, and stirs up fears of finality of Armageddon, in quite the same manner.[12]

No such sustained principled opposition to the tests could be expressed in Pakistan. There, despite a few brave voices on the streets, the fervent nationalist, anti-Indian outcry seemed to be unrestrained, a further proof of how little any genuine democracy had taken root. Jingoistic advocates of nuclear rearmament in New Delhi would hasten to claim that this ferment across the border justified their own action. Long-time backers of Pakistan in Washington or London, for that matter, might have shown some belated recognition of how dangerous their encouragement for these new forms of fascism could be. Having carried out their own tests and having noted how both Washington

and London seemed to be even more hostile to India than
they were themselves, Pakistan's nationalists embarked on
some other dangerous courses which dictatorial states can
unloose more readily than democratic ones. A series of fresh
terrorist attacks were made against Kashmir, eclipsing even
the horror of the Prankote massacre. Sharif recalled his
parliament to prepare the way to impose Sharia, the full-
scale, far-reaching Islamic law which even some of his predecessors had resisted. The nuclear crisis had already had
the effect of heightening all the other tensions. Would not
Sharif's resort to Sharia merely intensify Hindu extremism
across India in one form or another?

However, again something different happened. Indian
democracy kept its head, and its capacity to think and speak.
In 1998 Hiroshima Day, 6 August, saw bigger demonstrations in almost every Indian city than ever before:
300,000 marching through the pouring rain in Calcutta,
5000 in Delhi, thousands in Bangalore with many leading
Indian scientists at their head, 700 in Mumbai taking a
pledge at the Azad Maidan 'to work tirelessly for the complete elimination of nuclear weapons', cartoonist Abu Abra-
ham leading the Kerala demonstration; and, speaking at
many of these demonstrations, the one whose words have
epitomized best the new mood and the new spirit which
have swept afresh across the world: Arundhati Roy, author
of *The God of Small Things*, with her essay 'The End of
Imagination'.

Arundhati Roy's philippic against the nuclear bomb was
the most comprehensive ever delivered and as eloquent and
urgent as anything uttered by the founders of the movement
of protest fifty years before. She spoke with the insight and
passion of Bertrand Russell. She called the nuclear bomb
'the most anti-democratic, anti-national, anti-human, out-

right evil thing man has ever made'. And she proved the
case on every count. True, she did have a special Indian
context in which she wrote: 'India's nuclear bomb is the
final act of betrayal by a ruling class that has failed its
people.' Others beside the present rulers of India must bear
the responsibility. Her indictment did not spare Indira
Gandhi, who had given the orders for the first Pokhran
tests in 1974. She developed her attack into a full-scale
pacifist one; but there was no weakening in her argument.
She had already destroyed the so-called theory of deterrence more effectively than anyone before her: 'Flaw
Number One is that it presumes a complete sophisticated
understanding of the psychology of your enemy. It assumes
that what deters you (the fear of annihilation) will deter
them. What about those who are not deterred by that? The
suicide bomber psyche – the "We'll take you with us"
school – is that an outlandish thought? How did Rajiv
Gandhi die?' But no quotation can do justice to the urgency
of her summons: 'Let's not forget that the stakes they were
playing for are huge. The end of our children and our
children's children. Of everything we love. We have to
reach within ourselves and find the strength to think. To
fight.'[13]

The only matter with which Arundhati Roy did not deal
was the question how the fight against the bomb was to be
translated into international action. Previous Indian
governments had played a most honourable part in that
exertion, and the hope was still there that such an Indian
leadership could be restored.

Some people claim that the criticisms of the Indian Prime
Minister on this matter were too persistent and unfair. But
others could recall what he himself had said to the world at
large not so long before. He addressed the United Nations

General Assembly on 24 September 1998, but he had also addressed the same Assembly the previous year as India's foreign minister. His exact words then, on 4 October 1997, were as follows:

> We are told that nuclear weapons are a necessary deterrent against war and that it is only the assurance of their use that constitutes the core of deterrence. We do not accept that thesis. We believe nuclear weapons are dangerous whether they are in the possession of one country, some countries, or many countries. India is not a nuclear weapon state and has no intention of being one. India would not go in for nuclear weapons even if all the other countries in the world did so.

This quotation, prominently printed in the Indian press soon after the Prime Minister's speech in New York in October 1998, like the epigraph at the head of this book, illustrates afresh how genuine the freedom of the press in India could be and how determined brave men and women could be to exercise it.

Chapter 5

To the Non-Nuclear World

No: not despair precisely; when we know
All that can come, and how we meet it, our
Resources, if firm, may merit a more noble
Word than this to give it utterance.
            Byron, *Sardanapalus*

How to stop the India–Pakistan competition in insanity? How to lift the still legitimate fear of a nuclear accident? How to revive the momentarily blocked disarmament process? How to establish a world authority equipped to forbid the aggressions of the coming century? How to translate into action the admirable proposals of the Non-Aligned Movement – with maybe even some British assistance?

These are the real questions to which I will offer answers; but first we must confront other arguments which seem to require preferential consideration. Some of the top scientists or the top politicians, in various countries, insist that some later discoveries in death-dealing weapons demand even more urgent treatment. Once upon a time, for example, it was supposed that international provisions for dealing with poison gases of various kinds were widely accepted and had proved effective. This was a legitimate hope and the individual nations – Britain among them – which had worked to secure these first international compacts deserve full credit. Tragically for the world at large, however, it appears that the international control bodies have been outdone by the inventors of even more poisonous and penetrative gases. If indeed this is the latest horror which the scientists have developed for our affliction, we must search all the more earnestly for the international remedies which alone can save us. When United States cruise missiles bombed the Shifa chemical plant in Khartoum in August 1998, as a reprisal for the bomb blasts which destroyed American embassies in Kenya and Tanzania earlier that month, the American claim was that the factory managers, encouraged by experts from Iraq, had been manufacturing a chemical precursor to VX nerve gas. The Sudanese authorities persisted in their protest that the product was safely medicinal. Unfortunately, the outside world could never know the truth of these claims and counter-claims, since the American method of surprise bombing destroyed the evidence. How many hospital officials or innocent bystanders were killed in that raid is also a matter of guesswork; no one need believe the figures offered by any of the participants. However, even this question of common human decency which should concern us loses its significance in face of another. The American method of taking the law into their own hands is the worst way of seeking to establish respect for the kind of controls so necessary for the purpose. No maker of VX nerve gas anywhere on the planet will be deterred by what happened at the Shifa plant. A United Nations inspection team despatched before the raid would have been the right way to test the information which the American experts claimed to have at their disposal.

Somehow, the world's rulers – or perhaps we should restrict them in this reprimand to the rulers of the five nuclear states – seem content to adopt any new excuse to do nothing about the nuclear peril. Momentarily, the Indo-

Pakistan eruption shook them from their somnolence. Since both countries had gone ahead with tests against their will, and since it was evident that at least another half-dozen states would soon have the capacity to follow their example, it might have been imagined that 1998 would have been the year when the world community applied its mind afresh to the task of banishing the menace for ever. Each of the five has offered some excuse why they must turn to other concerns. President Yeltsin in Russia maybe had the best excuse for being distracted, although the nuclear aftermath in the former constituent territories of the Soviet Union is still the most menacing and neglected. President Jiang Zemin in Beijing has been the recipient of a 'good nuclear behaviour' certificate from President Clinton, although the value of the award may seem to have depreciated. China, along with France and Britain, is also a signatory of the CTBT, the instrument which forbids the fresh testing of nuclear weapons and thereby also helps to prevent their proliferation. France, having attracted considerable odium in conducting some new 'final' tests in someone else's country in 1996, none the less joined Britain in being the first to ratify the CTBT in April 1998. In 1998 Britain produced a new *Strategic Defence Review* which cut the number of nuclear warheads in commission by half but envisaged the maintenance of the nuclear element in our defences for the next thirty years, and made no reference whatever to the economies which might follow more general nuclear disarmament.[1] We shall return to this omission shortly.

Meanwhile, in the two last weeks of August, a mid-summer madness seemed to take possession of the ruler of the most powerful of the five nuclear states. Indeed, even without America's nuclear arsenal, the commander-in-chief

of the American military machine has at his disposal a range
of modern weapons which means that, if challenged, he can
lash out at his enemies across continents with deadly effect
and with hardly any fear of reprisal. His country's enemies,
well aware of this, sometimes develop ingenious new
methods of warfare of their own. Sometimes, fascinated by
the nuclear argument, they look for that protection too.
Hence the moves in this direction in countries where the
Americans or the world at large might find such inclinations
especially frightening – Iran, Iraq, Libya, North Korea.
Each of these would like to follow the example of Pakistan,
which may indirectly have helped them. Pakistan, indeed,
takes up a position of peculiar equivocation in the nuclear
debate. It permits American flights across its territory to
hit (or rather miss) Islamic targets in Afghanistan. It has
scientific knowhow of its own to dispense, albeit acquired
from China or Korea. It declares holy war against India,
but not against the United States. At any moment, the
tottering regime in Islamabad might move closer to the
more purposeful regime across the Afghanistan border
which has clearer ideas and would be glad to get its hands on
Pakistan's nuclear test fields. Quite contrary to the benign
prophecies of the nuclear club apologists, even at the time
of the Indo-Pakistan tests, the pressure in other states to
acquire these weapons is becoming stronger, not weaker.
President Clinton sought to justify his August raids on
targets in the Sudan and Afghanistan on the grounds that
he was fighting terrorism. It is certainly necessary for the
international community or individual states to fight and
defeat terrorism, but this requirement must not be allowed
to block or delay plans for the abolition of nuclear weapons.
Suppose that terrorists were to acquire nuclear weapons; it
is not at all a fanciful suggestion – indeed, this is one of

the possibilities which has been especially studied in the United States. It requires much more rigorous, urgent and comprehensive scrutiny than it has yet been accorded.

The summer of 1998 offered the clearest illustration of how our nuclear-encompassed world should not conduct its affairs. It is hard to conceive of a doctrine more menacing for our future peace than the American misinterpretation of Article 51 of the United Nations Charter, the right to self-defence. In no language does self-defence mean the right to indiscriminate retaliation. Indeed, a Security Council resolution passed without dissent in 1964 specifically condemned reprisals as 'incompatible with the purpose and principles of the United Nations'. Yet, without the slightest effort to secure Security Council sanction, the Americans drove their cruise missiles through this particular clause, indeed through the whole fabric of international law. The excuse for their action was that all peace-loving nations must unite to fight terrorism, especially the kind of terrorism which had been so wantonly unleashed against the American embassies in Kenya and Tanzania. The plea itself is indisputable. We shall need stronger laws and stronger police forces to protect American lives and many others. But the way to fight terrorism is not to become terrorists ourselves, which is what the Americans did become in their counter-attacks against the Sudanese and the Afghans in that midsummer. One of the worst aspects of modern terrorism is the perpetrators' apparent disregard for the innocent bystanders, men, women and children, they may involve in their atrocities. But just such innocent bystanders were maimed and killed when the Americans bombed targets in the Sudan and Afghanistan – not so many as were murdered in the American embassies but, none the less, innocent spectators; and, since they hadn't killed so many, the American experts quickly announced that they would soon be doing it again.

The passage of American missiles across Pakistan had an irony all its own. It was a monstrously illegal use of Pakistan airspace and, if Pakistan's complicity in the operation were detected by its normally friendly neighbours in the north, it could provoke violent retaliation from the same bunch of terrorists the American bombs were supposed to exterminate. So intricate were these military-cum-diplomatic developments that the Americans despatched an air marshal to warn Pakistan. Somehow he found the mission impossible to fulfil, and had to deliver the warnings after the actual passage of the missiles. However, he was able to carry out one part of his instructions: to make it clear to the Pakistanis that the missile was American, not Indian. If the Indian authorities had been held guilty of the same offence, they could have set the whole sub-continent ablaze with nuclear flashes.

World-wide terrorism is the latest excuse used by the leading powers, headed by the United States, to delay action on nuclear matters. It is deemed more urgent to seek a solution to the allegedly more insistent problem posed by the terrifying power which the terrorists have acquired. A truly terrifying threat it is; but it is not so novel as the Americans find it convenient to suggest, and not one to be combated by becoming terrorists ourselves in our readiness to break the law or our callousness about innocent victims. Attempts to destroy terrorists by terrorist methods might not only misfire, as they frequently do, but might also fortify the most dangerous among the targets. President Reagan's bid to kill Libya's leader, Colonel Qadhafi, by a raid launched illegally from British soil killed some innocent bystanders but left him stronger than ever. Once, Fidel

Castro in Cuba was Washington's terrorist Number One; maybe the new monster figure in Afghanistan, Osama bin Laden, will prove equally agile in escaping the American vengeance. Who knows, his training with the CIA might have taught him a few tricks. Whoever the terrorists are, the idea of terrorists with the bomb could be the ultimate threat. However, some American experts have examined this prospect from another angle: for it could be the most conclusive reason of all for effective international control as the only remedy. However, there are some other, still more urgent perils we must examine first.

Seen through the eyes of the supposed great powers' rebukes for India and Pakistan – with the United States giving the lead, but with most of the rest sycophantically following – the American policy might be accepted, whatever its other failings, as the best for stopping the spread of nuclear weapons. If that had been the case, it could be forgiven many shortcomings. But in the case of India and Pakistan, it may have helped to produce exactly the opposite effect to that desired. In this context the exceptions eclipsed the rule. The absence of a consistent principle at the heart of the policy put many aspects of its application in jeopardy. Even before the India–Pakistan fiasco, the failures inherent in the US approach were evident in several other fields. How is the balance to be held in the future when the exposure of nuclear horrors seems to grow ever more threatening and the demands of responsible people in search of practical remedies ever more insistent? The military experts have often refused to recognize the scale of the first challenge, and we nuclear disarmers may have neglected the second. We must bring the two together.

The Americans have at their disposal an instrument which can still be most helpful in moving towards a truly non-nuclear ideal. The International Atomic Energy Authority was something of an American creation, but it is by no means merely an American creature. According to the statutes on which it was established in 1954, its founders always envisaged that it could play a major part in the work of disarmament. As we have noted before, the more President Eisenhower applied his military judgement to the matter, the more he was convinced that safety must be finally sought along that road. A curious variety of other American authorities have been forced to the same conclusion. It was the idea behind the Baruch Plan of 1946 which could have stopped the race before it started. However, that proposed control scheme was left so effectively in American hands that few observers were surprised when the Soviet leaders of the time rejected it. Another quite unexpected American sponsor of such a genuine international scheme was John Foster Dulles, who seemed in his public declarations always to be advocating a system of absolute American hegemony. But recently declassified material has revealed that at one period in the mid-1950s he presented a memorandum to President Eisenhower proposing a fundamental change. Atomic power was 'too vast a power to be left for the military use of any one country'. He proposed therefore 'the transfer of control over nuclear forces to a vetoless United Nations Security Council'. A pity this secret, first recorded in Robert McNamara's book published in 1994, was not made public much earlier; it could at least have provoked a much wider debate.[2] The Aldermaston marchers of the late 1950s might have contrived a special banner for Dulles' benefit. What Eisenhower did bequeath to us in his International Atomic Energy Authority was a body which could both keep track of world-wide developments in nuclear weapons and offer the prospect of foolproof inspection systems in the end, if and when the world made up its mind to come to its senses. The nuclear race has in some places, and not only in the Indian sub-continent, been intensifying; the peril must be properly reported. But even as we report it, we may also note that the instruments of inspection which expose the horror can also help to point the road back to safety.

Most directly, the International Atomic Energy Authority has been used as one of the instruments to monitor the operation of the Non-Proliferation Treaty, which came into force in 1970 and was renewed in 1995. Along with the Test Ban Treaty, first signed in 1963, it is the only agreed mechanism to hold in check the spread of nuclear weapons. Without the check it has imposed, but more especially without the development of systems of inspection, the world would be a much more dangerous place than it is. However, the NPT has serious deficiencies. As we have already noted, it favours the position of the five nations which possessed the nuclear capability at the time of its signature in 1970; that was why many countries, India among them, refused to sign. To some degree the five leading nuclear powers recognized this discrimination and sought to offer an escape from it, explicitly indicating in the preamble that they contemplated moving to 'the liquidation of all their existing stockpiles, and the elimination from national arsenals of nuclear weapons and the means of their delivery'. True, no exact timetable was specified in the document; but the sense of urgency is still there. Many of the hundred-odd nations who did sign legitimately argue that they did so because they took the preamble at its word and saw the NPT as the prelude to the full-scale, world-wide disarmament also specified in that same treaty. India subscribed to these long-term goals – no nation did so more honestly and steadfastly – but Indira Gandhi, the country's Prime Minister at the time, would not sign the treaty; for, as we have seen, it introduced the proposition that some nations (including China) could be trusted with nuclear weapons and others (including India) could not. What Indian leader could accept such a doctrine? Moreover, with or without direct Chinese aid, soon after the 1970 war with India, Pakistan had started its own secret nuclear weapons programme. The first actual scientific steps were taken in India at the same time, and each might say that the move on the other side of the border was what made its own move inevitable. Whatever its virtues, and even leaving India aside, the NPT has suffered some serious failures. It is necessary to examine the reasons for these in particular cases, and to examine too where aspirants to join the nuclear club may still be looking for assistance and encouragement. The NPT was supposed to put an end to all such manoeuvres, and clearly it has not.

Nine nuclear countries have appeared on the published lists. As of 1995, the following possessed nuclear weapons: Russia (11,000 warheads); the United States (8500); Ukraine (1500); France (800); Kazakhstan (600); China (300); the United Kingdom (300); Israel (100); and Belarus (36). Four of these – Russia, Ukraine, Kazakhstan and Belarus – were once part of the Soviet Union. Each of them, headed by Russia itself, has accepted some form of inspection under the disarmament agreements reached with the United States. Each of them may be encountering such hideous problems in the process of dismantling that they would be only too glad to transfer their responsibilities to an international supervisory body – the sooner the better for the rest of us too, as we shall see later. All the others should be prepared to do the same. China might offer the most serious resistance; no invitation has been offered there. But what about Israel? Ever since the 1960s Israel has been developing a nuclear potential, at first with direct French assistance and later no doubt with American connivance. Both the timing and the scale of Israel's nuclear developments are better known than those of any other would-be nuclear power, although no open acknowledgement of them has been made, either by Israeli leaders or by their American suppliers; we glanced at the 'Israel Syndrome' in its Indian connection a little earlier. The whole matter must be brought into the open. Quite a number of Israeli leaders and American Presidents must have been jointly involved in plain breaches of the NPT. If they are to be allowed such a dispensation, how feeble will be the discipline to be applied elsewhere!

The case of Iraq presents itself, although in a rather different context. Iraq's desire and capacity to develop nuclear weapons were among the reasons why international action, led by the United States but supported eventually by the United Nations itself, was taken against the country to stop such work proceeding. It does appear that, in this respect at least, the action has succeeded, a success which includes a brilliant triumph for the inspection systems themselves. If the UN operations have indeed helped to achieve this result, we may all breathe a little more freely. Sooner or later, the same doctrine must be applied by the international community across the whole planet. It cannot be left to the Americans to pick and choose how and where the NPT is applied. That would be just another way of returning to the nuclear anarchy of the 1960s: every country for itself in this naked nuclear wilderness. That, after all, was the fatal Thatcher doctrine which may have helped to mislead both Saddam Hussein in Iraq and Binyamin

Netanyahu in Israel. Neither is fit to have a finger on any nuclear trigger. And once we stop to think, nor is anyone else. That is now the Robert McNamara doctrine too, as we shall reveal in a moment. A genuine Non-Proliferation Treaty must cover all countries and all weapons; despite the eloquent preamble, we are still far from achieving that ideal. But it would be just as foolish to suppose that nothing has been achieved, that the successes of the international community, so arduously secured, should be spurned and cast aside. A number of particular nations which it might be thought would wish to develop nuclear initiatives have turned the other way – Argentina, Brazil, South Africa, some of the states previously in the Soviet Union. An orderly dismantling of existing nuclear installations will require international action, and the more this is seen as a world-wide programme, the less local prides or sensibilities may be injured in the process.

Some years ago, after the break-up of the Soviet Union, it was supposed that the most serious aspect of this development might be interference with the systems of control. When political direction from Moscow became shaky or uncertain, to whom would submarine captains or missile engineers turn for their orders? Who could be sure that the orderly systems of control would still be effective? Richard Norton-Taylor, examining the question in the *Guardian*, concluded bravely that 'Russia's nukes are safer than they look.' He did his best to describe how the present system works.[3]

Nothing like safe dispositions can be said to have been established in the territories previously comprising the Soviet Union. As noted above, four of the successor states came into possession of nuclear warheads – Russia, Ukraine, Kazakhstan and Belarus. President Yeltsin might insist that his 11,000 warheads, all fully tested, are under proper surveillance, but the warnings of his predecessor, Mikhail Gorbachev, apply even more acutely. In Belarus's neighbour Georgia, control was sufficiently shaky to persuade President Clinton and Prime Minister Blair to offer a helping hand with a transfer of some waste for storage to the safe hideout at Dounreay in Scotland. This was claimed by our Mr Blair as a necessary act of international co-operation, and so for sure it was intended to be; more such gestures will be needed in the future.

When Blair made his offer about the safe haven which Dounreay could supply, he must obviously have been speaking on the basis of some scientific evidence offered him at the time, but the mere name should have warned him to be more cautious. Scottish nuclear disarmers had long been protesting about the operations at Dounreay, and naturally renewed their clamour both at the time of Blair's announcement and when the actual cargoes from Georgia were flown in a few weeks later. A few more months passed and the ministers responsible in the government, in both Scotland and London, reached the conclusion that Dounreay itself must be closed. The process would take years and would cost £10 billion to complete. But whatever the cost, all those responsible were no doubt immensely relieved that the decision had been made – a decision forced by the appearance of a Health and Safety Commission report not only describing some chronic failures of management in the past but faithfully reporting too what would be the cost of making the place safe in the future. Many such unpalatable prophecies and recommendations come out of the Health and Safety Commission. Sometimes their warnings were neglected. Dounreay may earn its fame as the place where action was taken just in time.

At Chernobyl, where the most fearsome of all the world's nuclear accidents occurred in 1986, the decommissioning process has not even started, twelve years later. All the experts, both in the Ukraine administration and in the international Chernobyl Consortium, which includes American participation, know what must be done. British Nuclear Fuels (BNFL) recently won the £10 million contract to start the work. The expert knowledge which British scientists and engineers have acquired, directed in the final resort by the near-independent Health and Safety Commission, can serve us all in the coming century. Maybe we should rechristen the BNFL the British Nuclear Finishing Laboratory, ready to be despatched at short notice to all afflicted trouble spots. Backed, if necessary, in particular instances by the findings of the Health and Safety Commission, the work of the new BNFL could lead the way in offering world-wide assurance that nuclear arsenals were being dismantled and no cheating was being tolerated. For members of a previous Labour government this development would be especially welcome since we insisted, when we established the Commission, that it must cut across all vested interests both in industry and in Whitehall, and must have the proper resources to achieve in the twentieth century what the Factories Acts achieved in the nineteenth. Among the vested interests we had to fight was the House of Lords, which voted against some of the best clauses in the bill. Moreover, soon after Labour lost the 1979 election, the Commission was starved of adequate resources. None the less, the work was properly started – as witness the latest report on Dounreay.

Chernobyl conjures up one portrait of the nuclear age. Nothing else, we must hope, compares in present horror or future menace with what is happening in Kazakhstan today. Between 1949 and 1989 470 tests were carried out there, 118 of them above ground, to produce the 600 warheads listed above. A report in the *Guardian* by Claudia McElroy illustrates afresh what we should never have forgotten: that the particular fiendishness of the nuclear weapon is how it continues to inflict its wounds on future generations. Gulzhan Smagulova grew up in the 1960s believing

> that the 'earth quakes' which regularly shook her house on Saturday mornings – making the furniture crash and the walls crack – were simply a necessary part of Soviet 'research'. Even when her neighbour bore a severely deformed child, and her own mother died prematurely from a combination of chronic health problems, she did not imagine that as many as 500,000 people in and around her home town Semipalatinsk (Semey) in north-east Kazakhstan were being exposed to radiation.
>
> Now, nine years after the last nuclear bomb was exploded at the Semey testing ground and the veil of cold-war secrecy was finally lifted, she can scarcely believe how little is being done to help the victims of what she calls 'a hidden war against our own people'. 'The test site may be silent, but the environmental and health problems are still massive,' she said. 'Because Semey is in such a remote part of the country, the government treats it as a leper colony. What's out of sight is out of mind. The most urgent issue now is to mobilise resources to help these victims improve their lives and learn to survive by themselves.' Ms Smagulova, a teacher, suffers skin disorders and high blood pressure, which she believes are due to radiation. The consequences of 40 years of radioactive contamination of land, water and food are hard to measure but the frequency and fatality rate of cancer, cardiovascular illness and mental illness have increased dramatically. In the village of Kainar, doctors said that 90 per cent of the 1029 patients examined between

1992 and 1993 had Aids. The infant mortality rate is said
to have tripled, and babies continue to be born with
deformities.

The Gorbachev era brought into existence numerous
civil and human rights groups, including the Nevada–
Semey anti-nuclear movement (named after the main US
and USSR testing sites), founded by the leading Kazakh
poet and politician Olzhas Suleimenov. The movement rallied huge public support, leading to the Semey site's closure
in 1981 by President Nursultan Nazarbayev of Kazakhstan.
Yet in a country struggling to cope with post-Soviet economic collapse, social transformation and abject poverty, the
government is more concerned with luring Western oil, gas
and mineral companies into the area than with the environ-
mental rehabilitation of one of its remotest regions.

At the same time it is spending huge amounts on a new
capital in the isolated northern city of Aqmola, for reasons
which remain opaque. President Nazarbayev, a product of
the Soviet system and reputedly the eighth richest man in
the world, 'won' the 1991 elections as sole candidate, and
has maintained his position by a referendum in advance
of elections due in 2000. Despite recent formation of an
opposition alliance, most observers believe he will neither
face nor tolerate any serious challenge. Mr Suleimenov was
dispatched to Italy as ambassador two years ago. Without
him the Nevada–Semey movement has effectively collapsed. 'It is not profitable for the state to advertise the
continuing crisis of the nuclear tests,' said Yuri Kuidin, a
veteran anti-nuclear campaigner and photographer, who has
just published a book of harrowing photographs of the continuing suffering in the region. 'Even if the government
wants to help it can't afford it, so it has really abandoned
hundreds of thousands of people.' His book shows children
born without arms, some with enormous hydrocephalic
heads, others blind and disfigured with tumours. 'I hope
my book will move people both locally and internationally

to make sure this issue is kept alive.' It's immoral just to abandon these people. 'Nuclear testing is still going on at Lop Nor in China, not too far from the Kazakhstan border and just last year saw the same deformities and radiation sickness there.' Russia, which many blame for the tragedy, has its own economic crisis and is reluctant to help. Few international aid agencies appear to have given much priority to the Semey region, some citing the difficulty of getting accurate health statistics and the country's multitude of socio-economic problems. Ms Smagulova believes that foreign companies in Kazakhstan should take the lead in providing funds for Semey, and she is lobbying for financial support for a disabled children's home in the town. 'They have money and ultimately it would be good for their image. Once the first step is taken, hopefully others will follow.'[4]

Kazakhstan ought to be a name among nuclear horrors to equal any of the others. This was a slightly later report sent from the same place, published in the *Observer*:

A United Nations Report to be published this month said that 1.2 million people around the test site are believed to have been affected by radiation, 100,000 of them directly. At the Health Department the Director listed the appalling statistics: huge rises in breast cancer over the past five years and a fall in the average age of sufferers from 40 to 25. More babies born with genetic abnormalities and more children suffering from stunted growth. Cancer rates of 270 per 100,000 population compared with 150 elsewhere in the country. TB cases twice the national figure. 'We don't really know enough about what we are dealing with,' said Tuletayeb. 'Who knows what else will emerge?'[5]

Nothing to equal that in the threat to our common humanity. So most of us would like to conclude; and yet another report had already appeared which stressed a characteristic of nuclear weapons often neglected or suppressed. In a sense the idea of an accidental nuclear war is even more hideous than that of one unloosed by some racist maniac. If anyone thinks the scientists were talking rubbish, they should read the report: here is the summary published in *The Asian Age*.

The risk of an accidental nuclear attack, which would be 'the greatest disaster' in history, has increased since the end of the Cold War, according to a study in the *New England Journal* of *Medicine*. 'The US and Russian arsenals remain on high alert,' said the report. 'This fact, combined with the ageing of Russian technical systems, has recently increased the risk of an accidental nuclear attack.' The study was done by Physicians for Social Responsibility, the US affiliate of International Physicians for the Prevention of Nuclear War, recipient of the 1985 Nobel peace prize.

The authors said such an accidental attack would create a 'public health disaster of unprecedented scale', and that prevention of this should be a global priority. Although both the United States and Russia agreed in 1994 not to aim nuclear missiles at each other, a nuclear missile could still be launched quickly, and some systems are designed to automatically 'launch on warning', the researchers said. 'There have been numerous "broken arrows" (major nuclear-weapons accidents) in the past, including at least five instances of US missiles that are capable of carrying nuclear devices flying over or crashing in or near the territories of other nations,' the study said. The authors said that any nuclear arsenal is susceptible to an accident, and this could affect any of the declared nuclear powers – the United States, Russia, France, Britain and China – or undeclared powers including Israel, India and Pakistan. However, the report also said that 'the combination of the massive size of the Russian nuclear arsenal (almost 6000 strategic warheads) and growing problems in Russian control systems makes Russia the focus of the greatest current concern.' It also said some analysts are concerned that computer defects in the year 2000 could cause further problems in Russian nuclear controls. 'Both countries' official line is that the Russian controls are still good,' said Mr Bruce Blair, one of the authors of the study. 'I urge you to be sceptical.' In the United States, the study said 66,000 military officials involved in nuclear operations had to be removed from their posts, 41 per cent for alcohol or drug abuse. An accidental 'intermediate' launch from a Russian submarine would result in more than 6.8 million deaths in firestorms in eight cities in the United States. Millions of others would be exposed to harmful radiation. 'Almost certainly, this accident would lead to an all out nuclear war,' said co-author Ira Helfand. 'It would be the greatest disaster that we have ever known.'

The report concluded that anti-missile defences are inadequate protection and the best way to end the threat is an agreement to remove all nuclear missiles from alert status and eliminate rapid-launch capability. 'The United States should make it the most urgent national public health priority to seek a permanent, verified agreement with Russia to take all nuclear missiles off high alert and remove the capability of a rapid launch.'[6]

If any prospect could be more alarming than this, it is probably that of the terrorist group or individual with a nuclear weapon in their hands. The Indians, via the Americans, have recently been informed on this subject too. The following article, which appeared in *The Times of India* in December 1997, was pertinently subtitled 'A Clear and Present Danger'. The whole piece should be read and reread. It provides an expert American view on what has *not* been done to meet the terrorist threat defined by President Clinton.

In the testimony given by the House of Representatives International Relations Committee on global terrorism and organised crime on October 1 1997, the Director of the Federal Bureau of Investigation, Mr Louis Freeh stated that the possibility of international criminal elements dealing and trafficking in such suitcase weapons was taken seriously by various US law enforcement agencies. He characterised that possibility and the threat of that as extremely high and something which occupied much attention, not just from the criminal law enforcement point of view but from the national security point of view. 'If you can buy, as we saw two years ago, 2.7 kilograms of weapons-grade uranium or plutonium in Munich or Prague, the same channels of access for those materials could quickly or easily lead to a fully operational device,' he argued.

These disclosures reveal that there are weapons in nuclear weapon countries outside the defence arsenals which are very mobile and man-portable. In future, the dangers of nuclear proliferation are not likely to be in terms of use of nuclear weapons in regular interstate wars between armed forces of countries but in terrorist use of man-portable weapons. It is noteworthy that today a greater threat to international security is through the use of man-portable infantry weapons and not so much through high-calibre ones. Similarly, the nuclear weapon that is likely to be used will be more probably the man-portable one than the standard bomb or missile-borne warhead. The use of a nuclear weapon by way of aircraft-dropped bomb or a missile warhead can be traced to the aggressor and there can be retaliation. But a man-portable nuclear device exploded at the centre of a city will be difficult to be traced to a particular person or group. Let us imagine that the explosive device used in the World Trade Center or London financial district or Mumbai had been a two kiloton back-pack device instead of a few kilograms of conventional explosives. What would its impact have been on society?

The US authorities are aware of this threat. They have a system of Nuclear Emergency Search Teams (NEST) in the US to deal with such contingencies. The US is spending billions of dollars on counter-proliferation which is aimed at tracing such devices and their movements and to take steps to prevent such devices being used in the US. This is the real proliferation threat to the international community and there is a good case for the international community to address this threat collectively. But the US authorities do not want to focus on this threat. In a poll carried out under the auspices of the Henry L. Stimson Center, a majority of Americans found the prospect of terrorism against the US by terrorists smuggling nuclear weapons into the country as the most likely and the most frightening outcome of having nuclear weapons in the post-Cold War world.[7]

Looking back over the whole history of nuclear weapons, one aspect which stands out more starkly now than ever is the special brand of secrecy which the political leaders have sought to apply in this area, either on the instruction of their military chiefs or on their own initiative. During the Cold War crises which constantly threatened to turn into hot ones, such precautions may have seemed necessary on both sides. In the Soviet Union, in any case, secrecy was an essential part of the normal system of government. But democracies like Britain or the United States boasted of working on the basis of open covenants openly arrived at – or at any rate made public after a period designed to protect a nation's state security. However, these democratic preferences were often abandoned, and it seems they still are.

The United States government which professed to be so aggrieved at the secrecy practised by the Indian government on these questions is itself enforcing a level of secrecy quite as strict as any operated in the past and proposes to lead the world into the next century with the system still intact. Our own Labour government in Britain is not engaged in a nuclear enterprise on anything like the scale of the Americans; we have neither the will nor the capacity to do so. But we are sometimes infected by the demand for secrecy which nuclear arguments arouse. Successive Labour governments, I fear, have shown no taste for open government in this arena. After 1945, the decision to make the bomb was taken by Prime Minister Attlee and a few of his closest colleagues without any reference to the House of Commons. Ten years on, as we have seen, the party's leaders approved the next stage in the operation, and secured a mandate for it at the party conference. Twenty years later again another Labour government approved the latest modernization of the weapons. The new Labour government which came into office in May 1997 took up the reins having revoked all previous commitments which might appear to oblige it to take any form of unilateral action: as long as others kept nuclear weapons, we would keep ours. Not exactly a glorious stance, nor one likely to assist this country's appeal to others not to seek to join the nuclear club. However, the change of policy did achieve its immediate political purpose: the removal of this particular scare from the list of Conservative electoral accusations against the Labour party.

Still, unilateral action is not the only way to secure nuclear disarmament. Not even the most dedicated unilateralists have ever made such a claim. What is much more relevant in our present situation is to discover what progress the multilateralists have made in recent times and what they propose for the immediate future – or, to offer a little latitude, for the new century. As we have noted before, but without entering into a detailed scrutiny of the reasons for it, the policy-making of the five acknowledged nuclear powers often seems to have been afflicted by a paralysis, a complacent acceptance of the existing order of things, a toleration of present conditions for which there is no justification either in the nature of the weapons themselves or among the dozen or so states – a few more or a few less – who feel they have the right to join the club, and share its perils and protections.

We here in Britain, under our new government with its new electoral mandate, have a special duty to examine what is proposed. Both the details of present policy and a glimpse of a longer perspective were offered in the *Strategic Defence Review* presented to Parliament in July 1998 by the Secretary of State for Defence and the Foreign Secretary. It was not exactly the trumpet call which might have been expected from two such old-style nuclear disarmers as George Robertson and Robin Cook, but it is none the less a document which repays careful exegesis. The chapter directed to our primary concerns here is entitled 'Deterrence and Disarmament' and contains two striking illustrations which also curiously retain the balance between the two words in the chapter heading. One shows the Trident submarine HMS *Victorious* on trials, a vessel which, we are informed, 'can remain an effective deterrent for up to thirty years'. The other shows UN Special Commission (UNSCOM) weapons inspectors in Iraq, with a reminder below of how heavily arms control depends on effective international inspection and how British facilities at Aldermaston can offer special help in this work. So skilfully is the balance held between the two aspects of the title that it might be thought two different hands were at work. 'The Government', we are told at the start of the chapter, 'wishes to see a safer world in which there is no place for nuclear weapons'. *Good.* Progress on arms control is therefore an important objective of foreign and defence policy. *Better still.* Nevertheless, while large nuclear arsenals and risks of proliferation exist, our minimum deterrent remains a necessary element of our security. *Not so clear or clever.* Our insistence on our minimum deterrence might be one cause of the fresh proliferation which provokes the new fear. All the other nuclear powers – except the Americans, who, as we shall see, have a quite different programme – talk in terms of their minimum deterrent.

Having described the genuine reductions to be made in Britain's nuclear force – cutting it in half – the *Strategic Defence Review* returns in paragraph 70 to the awkward question about the future. On nuclear arms control the government hopes for further bilateral reductions in US and Russian strategic weapons through the Strategic Arms Reductions Treaty process. *So do we all.* It also hopes to see progress towards reducing the thousands of Russian shorter-range missiles. *And the shorter-range ones the Americans used against the Sudan and Afghanistan?* Our own arsenal, following the further reductions described above, is 'the minimum necessary to provide for our security for the foreseeable future and very much smaller than those of the other nuclear powers. Considerable further reductions in the latter would be needed before further reductions could become feasible.'

Taking it all in all, what does this mean? Nuclear Britain is here addressing the other nuclear powers and their lassitude or prevarication in addressing the problem. The Russians – the only ones mentioned by name: yes, we could get some progress there with the eager backing of multitudes of Russians. The Chinese and the French? It is hard to recall any recent occasion when either has been called upon to answer for its nuclear activities, although protests were still forthcoming from the places where they test their weapons. That just leaves the Americans among 'the latter' who would have to make 'considerable further reductions' before further British reductions would be 'feasible'. On this reckoning, we would keep our minimum deterrent for thirty years chiefly to deter the Americans, maybe also the Chinese and the French, but also a number of less reliable practitioners in the wider field previously described. Our *Strategic Defence Review* seems to view this prospect too calmly.

The best feature of the *Review* was the frequency with which the authors returned to the question of a greater openness, transparency, readiness to reveal nuclear secrets – as illustrated with the photograph of the United Nations inspectors performing their tasks on Iraqi soil. The more dangerous the developments in all kinds of weapons, the more necessary the development of infallible methods of inspection. Aldermaston holds secrets which, when fully divulged, may help to verify reductions across the whole field. The *Review* stresses that nations must learn to trust one another, that they must constantly test and improve the mechanisms required for the purposes of inspection and verification. Here, indeed, the new government was implementing a particular commitment which Robin Cook made on Labour's behalf before the election:

A new commitment to transparency by the nuclear weapons states: Confidence-building requires transparency and verification. As a starting point the nuclear weapons states should declare their existing inventories of plutonium and highly enriched uranium to the IAEA and open up to inspection their nuclear production facilities.

But that was just one of Labour's pre-election projects. In the same article Robin Cook also described several other initiatives in the nuclear field, none of which departed from Labour's commitment about the bomb, but each of which could surely help to change the international atmosphere.

> *Improved security assurances:* Labour has never accepted that the use of nuclear weapons against a non-nuclear weapons state could ever constitute a legitimate or rational act. The nuclear weapons states should jointly provide a new package of security assurances, including a commitment to 'no first use'.
>
> *Respect for nuclear weapons-free zones:* Regional nuclear weapons-free zones established by international agreement should be respected by the nuclear weapons states in peacetime. As envisaged in Article VII of the NPT, nuclear weapons-free zones are a powerful means of building confidence and easing the pressures that create the demand for nuclear weapons. Our security interests are served by encouraging their development, not flouting them.
>
> *Regular disarmament reports to the United Nations:* In order to sustain the momentum for disarmament, each of the nuclear weapons states should be obliged to lodge regular reports with the UN secretary general outlining what steps they have taken the fulfil their obligations under Article VI [of the NPT].
>
> *Negotiation of a nuclear weapons convention:* Standing negotiations should be opened with the ultimate objective of securing a convention banning the production and possession of nuclear weapons on the same lines as the recent international convention on chemical weapons. While not underestimating the enormity of the task and the long timescale it would require, such a forum could have a powerful symbolic role in establishing the elimination of nuclear weapons as the goal of diplomatic negotiation.[8]

If this formulation of Robin Cook's now smacks too much of the hustings, he could adopt instead the resolutions of the Non-Aligned Movement approved in Durban on 5 September 1998. Its declaration repeated the call for a programme of full-scale world-wide destruction of nuclear arsenals which it has made before, but proposed also the calling of a new disarmament conference before the end of the century to put the work in hand. To adopt his formula would be a nice compliment to President Mandela, and indeed to the many Indians who have used their democracy to challenge the policies of their government. The non-aligned countries criticized

the monopoly of the recognised nuclear weapon states in the right to own these weapons. They noted that the present situation, whereby nuclear weapon states insist that nuclear weapons provide unique security benefits and yet monopolise the right to own them, is highly discriminatory, unstable and cannot be sustained. They called for an international conference on nuclear disarmament, preferably in 1999, with the objective of arriving at an agreement before the end of the millennium, on a phased programme for the complete elimination of nuclear weapons. Anyone who objects that these are mere words should be reminded at once that the new Government in South Africa is the first in the world actually to abandon work to establish a nuclear capacity already in the process of achievement. Such a display of unilateral wisdom should have been acclaimed much more than it has been. It underlines afresh the wisdom and the honesty of NAM's new resolution which should win a special backing in new London.[9]

The present Labour administration, like previous Labour governments, is still committed to seek collective security on the widest scale. Often there have been raging arguments within the party on the gravest aspects of these questions; but often, too, there has been a grand convergence on a common policy to save the party and the country – 1919, 1940, 1945, 1974 and 1997. No one who surveys honestly the perils of our nuclear-threatened world could question that this remains the most inescapable summons of all.

President Clinton, or maybe his military–industrial complex which has survived from Eisenhower's day, has arrived at a different calculation of what his country might do in the coming century. Reports vary about the precise significance in nuclear terms if the programme proceeds; indeed, although the effects of such a programme would be global it has not been easy to extract reliable information about it. The most enlightening report came from Washington DC and appeared in the *Guardian*. The reporter was Ed Vulliamy, one of the great journalists of our age.

The United States is engaged in a massive secret programme to build a new generation of nuclear weapons, according to an internal US government document revealed yesterday. The document, a copy of which has been passed to the *Guardian*, exposes Washington to accusations that America has embarked on the design and development of new warheads using simulated detonations to evade the terms of the Comprehensive Test Ban Treaty. Among the weapons involved is the W-99 Trident missile, backbone of Britain's nuclear deterrent, which is being modernised to such an extent that the improved model will amount to a new 'Trident II'. The 300 page document – obtained by a physicist formerly of the secret Los Alamos nuclear laboratory – unveils a weapons programme which is, says Dr Matthew McKinzie, bigger than at the height of the cold war. The programme envisages growth of $4 billion (£2.5 billion) a year, compared with the equivalent of £3.7 billion during the cold war. The Stockpile Stewardship and

Management Plan, nicknamed the Green Book, is an internal report compiled by the energy department, which manages and maintains the nuclear arsenal. It was declassified and obtained by Dr McKinzie's Washington-based arms control monitoring group, the Natural Resources Defense Council, which is suing the government for breach of the test ban treaty. 'What we have is a massive nuclear programme,' Dr McKinzie said, 'which is a great deal larger than at the height of the cold war – which in the present security situation is staggering.'

The document shows the energy department and navy secretly underpinning work on new prototypes for nuclear weapons, and on improvements to existing warheads, two of which are the W-76 and W-88 missiles, fitted to the Trident submarine. Dr McKinzie says that the report shows the US government aiming to get round the test ban treaty by developing new weapons systems which do not need underground testing. 'The programme is trying to employ certain characteristics that five or six years ago would have needed underground testing. The question is are these missiles supposed to be deployed without needing to be tested in that way? This is happening just as the test ban treaty is going before the Senate for ratification.'

Dr McKinzie has written an analytical guide to the technically complex document, in which he explains that 'accurate theoretical models of the fundamental physical processes at work in each stage of a thermonuclear weapon's operation' can be used, 'therefore freeing future nuclear weapons design from the shackles of politically burdensome easily observed nuclear tests'. He goes on: 'If implemented over the next decade as planned ... the programme will seriously erode important non-proliferation objectives as well as undermine political assurances that the US government has provided for other nations.' Robert Bell, the director of arms control at the national security council, said last year that the effect of the test ban treaty was 'to rule out opportunities to create new weapons'. But the internal report talks about 'the development of advanced new types of nuclear weapons' and says that 'laboratories are currently working on programmes to provide new or modified designs' to nuclear weapons. Dr McKinzie said the work is intended to increase the power and precision of the next generation of weapons. The energy department said that the current programmes were concerned only with the modification and modernisation of existing designs. The head of the department's bomb-maintenance programme, Dr Victor Reis, said the work was 'wholly consistent with the goals of the test ban treaty'.[10]

Before any American President is allowed to proceed in this direction, the debate must be opened world-wide. The American military–industrial complex may hanker after a new age of military secrecy, but an even older American institution, the United States Constitution, protects the rights of free speech and the determination of brave men and women to exercise it. One of the most far-seeing of them, as mentioned earlier in these pages, I met at the Sixth Indira Gandhi Conference in New Delhi from 19 to 22 November 1997.

Robert McNamara, who from 1961 to 1968 was US Defense Secretary, supplied answers to all the questions posed at the head of this chapter and a few others equally pertinent for the survival of the human race. His statement naturally included some specific references to the Indian situation, but his aim was to lift these particular disputes to the international level where the long-term solutions are most likely to be found. Indeed, without this elevation we shall find ourselves thrust back into the old barren feuds. But once the objective of a non-nuclear world is restored, a whole range of new possibilities opens up before us. How to achieve the next beneficent stage in human development was what McNamara talked about in New Delhi. He himself did not always march behind Gorbachev's banner, but he never lacked good Russian auspices. At the end of his own book he quoted Andrei Sakharov on the subject: 'Reducing the risk of annihilating humanity in a nuclear war carries an absolute priority over all other considerations.'[11]

Ever since he had witnessed at first hand in the Cuban crisis the peril and the futility of nuclear weapons, McNamara had been an opponent of their use. He thought he had convinced the two Presidents he served – President Kennedy and President Johnson – of the same conclusion, though since the doctrine of the NATO alliance was that they would in certain circumstances use them, these doubts could not be made public. With the collapse of the Soviet Union and the possibility of much freer discussion with experts in Moscow and Cuba about what did happen in 1962, it became evident that the crisis had been even more dangerous than McNamara or anyone else involved had supposed. Both sides were misinformed about the movements of the other, and that misinformation could easily have been the cause of the ultimate disaster. One deduction which McNamara drew for himself more surely than ever was that human fallibility and nuclear weapons could not survive in the same world. Since there was no absolute foolproof, idiot-free cure for human failings, the weapons would have to go. Thereafter, he argued that case in season and out. Sometimes, he appeared to be winning; a number of military experts have seemed to come out on his side. But then other events would intervene to baulk such progress. He concluded his own book with these words: 'If we dare break out of the mind set that has guided the nuclear strategy of the nuclear powers for over four decades, I believe we can indeed "put the genie back in the bottle". If we do not, there is a substantial risk that the twenty-first century will see a nuclear tragedy.' His constant aim is 'a return by all five nuclear powers in so far as practicable to a non-nuclear world'. His proviso 'in so far as practicable' referred especially to the necessity of maintaining protection against break-outs or the acquisition of weapons by terrorists. The series of steps which he advocated to meet the objective must guard against this danger too. How to ensure that methods of surveillance and inspection could be brought to a pitch more nearly approximating perfection was one of the several aspects of the problem he was happy to discuss freely in New Delhi. It is, of course, a question of paramount importance on which some previous disarmament proposals have foundered. But it is true also that significant scientific advances have been made in this sphere. The terrorists' 'bombs in boxes' may look infinitely dangerous; but they too can be controlled if the world-wide will is allowed to prevail.

And yet we cannot honestly conclude with any such soft words of reassurance. Most of the previous crises in the world's nuclear history have not been attributable to the absence of sufficiently up-to-date mechanisms of communication and verification. All the most perilous decisions which forced the pace in the race at the worst moments were taken at the highest political level, and the remedies have to be sought there too. Sometimes and most appropriately these great governing decisions were taken at the Security Council of the United Nations, properly convened and properly instructed on the issues. Even so, as we know, the retention of the veto power for the five permanent members has meant the toleration of grievous wrongs, flagrant acts of aggression. Nevertheless, on several other occasions, from Korea in the 1950s to Iraq in the 1990s, the Security Council has acted in time with sufficient force. Had it not done so, our world would be an even more dangerous place. Still, no honest reporter of the scene can fail to report that at some moments of crisis there has been a perversion of the proper purposes of the Security Council to suit the requirements of the United States. No well-informed Indian observer – nor any well-informed Pakistan observer, for that matter – could accept that the United States had the right to apply sanctions as it did after the recent nuclear tests on the sub-continent. When India and Pakistan sought to put their respective cases they were unceremoniously told to shut up and take their orders. The resort to these gruff instructions was customarily excused on the grounds that this was the best way to stop the spread of the latest know-how about these terrible weapons. However, such admonitions always included the self-regarding claim that the five acknowledged nuclear powers must keep their monopoly into some unspecified future, and that the rest of mankind must accept this decree. As the argument developed in the autumn of 1998, especially at the meeting of the United Nations in New York, a fascinating divergence of outlook was seen to develop between Pakistan and India. Pakistan, being harder hit by the sanctions and the economic climate, seemed quite ready, as required by the Security Council, to sign the CTBT, even if it meant abandoning its claim to be a real nuclear power. India, on the other hand, still persisted in refusing to sign, partly at least on the grounds of principle stated by previous Indian leaders – not only on their own account, but generally on grounds of international policy. The aim – the only sane aim – was to use the present crisis to secure a much larger and longer-term system of control. However, so strong was

the American resistance to this form of development that
many of the most astute Indian observers of the scene saw
the US pressure, backed so sadly by the rest of the Security
Council, as a kind of trick, aimed at persuading or forcing
India and Pakistan to sign the CTBT without securing
any variations. That would mean that they were committed
forever to forgo any further moves along the nuclear road,
while the members of the nuclear club retained their monopoly. Such an outcome would also be regarded as insulting
to the non-aligned countries, headed by South Africa. It
would make the whole BJP Pokhran tests affair look ridicu-
lous. At one stage Secretary of State Albright was insisting
that both India and Pakistan sign the CTBT and NPT but
that neither would subsequently be considered a nuclear
power. What right she had to make such stipulations is not
clear. Neither she nor President Clinton had ever shown
much interest in Indian sensitivities.

The Americans claimed that they were trying to stop the
deadly proliferation. But however justified this excuse might
have been in the past, it clearly lacked force when, despite
all the warnings, both India and Pakistan felt themselves
justified in taking the next steps along the treacherous
nuclear path. If India and Pakistan could not be restrained
by American threats, what effect would such strictures have
for those countries that had elevated the United States to
the role of arch-enemy? How to stop Iraq, or North Korea,
or Libya, or Iran? The list is by no means exhausted. Indeed,
one of the troubles with the exercise of American hegemony
is the wide choice of chief devils to whom the most summary
treatment must be applied. One year it was Iran and another
it was Iraq; but when Iraq and Iran fought an eight-year
war of their own, it was not easy to see how the American
interest could be upheld. In none of these instances, pre-

sumably, could the 1998 Khartoum or Afghanistan remedy be applied: that is, direct attacks across international frontiers on targets selected by the American secret service. The proposition has only to be stated to prove its absurdity. In those instances when this course was taken, the few people who knew in advance what was proposed, headed by our own Prime Minister, should have stopped it. It was another stride down the road towards international anarchy.

How are we to restore – how to establish – a genuine international order, with the programme for the dismantling of the nuclear arsenals properly decreed and with a timetable? Nothing less will serve as an objective and what is needed now is a new sense of urgency. In so far as they are able to express their opinion, the vast majority of the human race have given their judgement on the matter. They have even put general resolutions on the subject on the Order Paper of the United Nations. For some incomprehensible reason our own government has failed to sign that document, but the oversight can easily be remedied. Our government has stated, in its official *Strategic Defence Review*, that it wants to live in a non-nuclear world. We should tell them that we want to speed up the process, to restore the timetable included in the Rajiv Gandhi's proposals of 1986 which envisaged the full-scale dismantling of the arsenals in the next ten years. A more effective United Nations with a remodelled Security Council is desperately needed to deal with a whole range of other problems. However, we must be vigilant in ensuring that the necessary constitutional reforms do not block all others.

A British government which had recovered its independent voice would be in an especially advantageous position to see that both aims were pursued at the same time – a more representative Council embracing those excluded for one reason or another in 1945, but still one which set a date for the fulfilment of the great power pledge on nuclear weapons. Two of the countries formerly excluded but obviously eligible now, Germany and Japan, would eagerly accept the nuclear commitment. Indeed, Japan might insist upon it. But the rest of Asia should also have a voice, and, until these latest nuclear controversies, it was always considered that India would be the best candidate to speak for them – to speak, indeed, for the whole non-aligned world, which once found its best spokesman in Prime Minister Nehru and now repeats the same urgent message in the accent of President Mandela. If the rulers of India, by their resort to the nuclear tests, turn out to have forfeited that claim, that deed was something worse than a crime: 'But yet the pity of it, Iago! Oh Iago, the pity of it, Iago!' And yet, by the time this book is printed, India's democracy may have restored India's reputation.

Robert McNamara's prospect of a non-nuclear world is challenged, as previous nuclear disarmers have been challenged, by the so-called realists, the experts on the subject who claim to have studied most closely the likely developments in the relationships between the so-called great powers following the collapse of the Soviet Union. Two of these who engaged in the argument with McNamara brought expert knowledge from different fields and different political stances, at least in the United States. One was Henry Kissinger, who had been Secretary of State in President Nixon's administration; the other was Zbigniew Brzezinski, National Security Adviser in President Carter's. Kissinger foresaw a future not so different from the eighteenth or nineteenth century, in which nations would be more prepared and able to balance their competing national interests. Brzezinski expressed another fear – that the lifting of the nuclear threat would encourage more wars waged by conventional weapons. But neither he nor Kissinger faced the reality which such figures as our own Field Marshal Lord Carver, Chief of Staff from 1973 to 1977, have done: an absolute refusal to assume that we should ever initiate the use of nuclear weapons. The power relationships recreated *à la* Kissinger could jostle us all to death.

Robert McNamara's own prophecy takes proper account of the interdependent world in which we live.

> No nation, not even the United States, can stand alone in a world in which nations are inextricably entwined with one another economically, environmentally and with regard to security. The United Nations Charter offers a far more appropriate framework for international relations in such a world than does the doctrine of power politics. It is that Charter properly backed which could have stopped the modern aggression against Kuwait, against Bosnia, against Rwanda, and prepared the way to take custody of the nuclear weapons themselves.[12]

It is a step-by-step process indeed; but one in which, thanks to CND, Gorbachev, Rajiv Gandhi, McNamara and a few others, we can now take some healthy great strides.

That is one way of finishing; but since we started with the poets, maybe the best way to end is with those who have often shown a greater sense of urgency than the rest of us. One such was Ursula Fanthorpe, whose representation of William Tyndale bore such a striking likeness to my own father.

> So little time. We have to hustle God
> Who, in His unhorizoned sphere of time,
> Can hardly know how short our seasons are.
> And I pray too for resurrection in the word.

This shall be written for those who come after.
And still, these tedious Chronicles waiting for me,
These kings and priests and rulers of this world,
These Jeroboams and Jehoiakims,
Between me and *beatus vir*, the happy man,
Whose leaf shall not wither. Unlike mine.
And look, whatsoever he doeth it shall prosper.
Et omnia quaecumque faciet prosperabuntur.
Prosperabuntur? God's teeth, what a word
For Christian tongues to wrestle with. Language for liars!
Our dear and patient English shall rip out
The rubbish Jerome stuffed in the Church's mouth.
I must get on. Day and Night. Instantly.
The Psalms are waiting. So are the English.
Vile the place is, but still my Father's house.
Lampless or not. He lights it.[13]

Appendix 1

Jonathan Schell's seminal book on this subject, *The Gift of Time: The Case for Abolishing Nuclear Weapons Now*, was published by Granta Books just when I was completing my own. I wrote a review of it which was recently published in the *Observer*. I publish an unedited version of that review here.

A REAL CASE FOR IMPEACHMENT

Campaigns for nuclear disarmament show a familiar pattern; they may rise suddenly to the highest pitch of excitement, but then relapse into a seeming slothfulness, as appears to be the situation now. Opponents of the whole idea have a ready explanation. Idealists of one breed or another may be responsible for the original hysteria, but then the practical men of action or, rather, no action, step forward to put a stop to all such tomfoolery. Whatever else is known or unknown, the absolute impossibility of getting the nuclear genie back into the bottle is there for all to see.

Jonathan Schell has his own reason for being fascinated by this phenomenon. At the time of the last swelling tide in favour of nuclear disarmament, on both sides of the Atlantic, in the early 1980s, his book *The Fate of the Earth* hit the mood and explained the facts better than anyone else's. No politician in charge would have any excuse for not knowing what would happen if he pressed the nuclear button. But, thanks to a whole range of factors, not excluding the reading of Jonathan Schell's book and the movement he helped to inspire, the world has seemed to draw back from that particular precipice. 'Whatever else you do, don't take that course; you'll bring on your own people horrors even worse than those inflicted on the cities of Hiroshima and Nagasaki.' At one stage that truth struck President Reagan, and it put the whole NATO strategy in jeopardy.

Not that the great powers, the five members of the nuclear club, have taken anything like the necessary precautions which the atmosphere of the 1980s or their own treaty obligations demanded. Each of the five has its own excuse for the failure and each cites the others as part of their apologia. Our own right little, tight little island, having cut the programme in half, still proposes to keep 150 warheads sailing round our shores on a hair trigger alert. If that sounds so safe, with our solid English hands on the tiller, what about the Chinese, say, or the Russians, who may be conducting operations no less legitimate than ours, according to their present international obligations, but still infinitely dangerous? According to the recent *Dispatches* programme on Channel Four, the Chinese government still has a full-time job on its hands explaining the horrific, persistent, radioactive effects of their 1960 tests or some more recent ones. Did Tony Blair mention the matter on his recent trip to Beijing or President Clinton on his more extensive tour? The accommodations offered to China by her fellow club members seem to exceed anything required by diplomatic manners. They indicate an acceptance of the permanence of nuclear weapons, however much this may involve broken promises to the rest of the world or broken bodies in the places where their experiments are conducted.

China is indeed the example quoted by the most brilliant of the advocates of the bomb in Schell's book. Fred Charles Iklé speaks with the tongue of angels but is drawn back in every argument to the same devilish conclusion. I cite the case to show what previous readers of Schell's books already know. He is not looking for any easy answers. He searches remorselessly for the truth that can save mankind.

But here let me declare an interest, as Members of Parliament sometimes do when it suits them. I too over these recent months have been seeking to complete a book on the subject. I had not the pleasure of a meeting with the incorrigible Mr Iklé. But I did meet at a seminar in New Delhi another of Schell's principal witnesses: Robert McNamara, once at a most critical moment in world history the United States Secretary of Defense, but now a nuclear disarmer as passionate as any Aldermaston marcher. Many of the late night arguments we had in New Delhi – it was before the Indians let loose their own particular brand of nuclear lunacy – always seemed to return to the question of how reliable the latest system of inspection could be. McNamara has specialised in this aspect of the subject but he has his own grave warning for a longer future: nuclear weapons of all brands or breeds are too dangerous to be left in man's fallible hands. One day there will be another accident to out-Chernobyl Chernobyl.

No one, I believe, can listen to McNamara and not conclude that the world's leaders would be convinced, if only they would listen. But then Jonathan Schell brings to the witness box an even more newly dedicated nuclear disarmer. General George Lee Butler, the last commander of the United States Strategic Air Command before it was incorporated into an even more prestigious body, was originally a professor of nuclear subjects at the Air Force Academy and then at the highest level in the Pentagon, the man who would have to pass on the orders from the President. The more he saw, the stronger became his determination to

work for disarmament, indeed, total abolition. Talk of a
Daniel come to judgement! He could soon have all the
Pentagon lions leaping to his orders. The eighteen pages
in Schell's book devoted to the Butler interview are as eloquent and conclusive as anything ever written on the subject. 'Nuclear weapons are irrational devices. They were
rationalised and accepted as a desperate measure in the face
of circumstances that were unimaginable. Now as the world
evolves rapidly, I think that the vast majority of the people
on the face of the earth will endorse the proposition that
such weapons have no place among us. There is no security
to be found in nuclear weapons. It is a fool's game.'

Nothing could be plainer: 'It is simply wrong, morally
speaking, for any mortal to be invested with the authority
to call into question the survival of the human race.' And
yet, as Schell also testifies, there is one place in the United
States where the moral has not been understood. His book,
which concludes with Butler's testimony, starts with the
declaration by President Clinton in the White House on the
same subject – the so-called Presidential Decision Directive
issued in early December 1997 envisaged the unrestricted
retention of nuclear weapons by the United States. Instead
of the plain English of General Butler's declaration, the
President and his nuclear advisers prefer a gobbledegook
of their own which, however, indisputably insisted that the
policy of nuclear deterrence remained in force and would
do so for an unspecified future. President Clinton's content-
ment with this situation is a scandal all on its own.

Some previous American Presidents have applied their
mind to the problem more humanely and far-seeingly,
which is one reason why the peril has been scotched, but
not yet killed. President Clinton shows no interest or understanding of the international law which must be established

and respected if the spread of nuclear weapons is to be checked. How to stop the terrorists getting their hands on the nuclear secrets, and indeed the weapons themselves, is one of the most intricate questions discussed in Schell's book. It won't be done by American Presidents who take the law into their own hands to bomb where they please on the just or the unjust, and in the same breath unloose a Presidential Decision Directive claiming absolute nuclear power from here to eternity.

Robert Bell, a member of Clinton's National Security Council, offered this bleak comment on the President's policy. It would mean keeping nuclear weapons as the corner-stone of the nation's defence 'for the indefinite future'. Such a contemptuous abandonment of America's international commitments might win favour among Clinton's die-hard Republican opponents, but not with the rest of humanity, as defined by General Butler. Indeed, considering the issue at stake, this Directive so carelessly published could constitute a real case for impeachment.

Appendix 2

Critics of CND sometimes protested that the case presented outside was not carried to the House of Commons. This was not so. I recall the speeches on the subject in the 1950s and 1960s by Emrys Hughes and Sydney Silverman, two of the best parliamentarians of their generation, apart from their other virtues. Two decades later Bob Cryer was the one who put the case best. Here was one of my own contributions, in response to the activities of Harold Macmillan as Prime Minister, as described in chapter 2.[1]

Mr Michael Foot (Ebbw Vale):   It would be tempting for me to follow the argument of the hon. Gentleman the Member for Gravesend (Mr Kirk) in his references to the Common Market and the present negotiations, particularly since I take a view strongly opposed to that which he adduced. It is, however, interesting that the hon. Gentleman should now discover – and I do not say that he had not realised it partially before – that there is a considerable question – and it may be that the hon. Gentleman's visit to Poland has done him some good – as to whether the Common Market is not going to intensify the division of Europe rather than assist in removing that division.

The hon. Gentleman appears to have come to appreciate that there is a growing difference of opinion on this matter among people who know a lot about how German policy is directed and the ends it seeks to secure. However, I congratulate the hon. Gentleman on the candour of the first part of his reference to this matter.

He said clearly that the economic aims of the Common Market were subordinate to the political aims, although the Leader of the Liberal Party did not seem absolutely clear on that point. If we are to go into the Common Market – and I am opposed to it – we should do so with our eyes open, knowing exactly what is proposed. Indeed, the hon. Gentleman quoted some of the proposals for setting up a European Parliament which would govern these affairs.

I have never been able to remove from my mind something that was said by the Lord Privy Seal during our debate on the Common Market a few months ago, when the right hon. Gentleman made some reference to the method by which a Parliament for Europe might be composed. He made the suggestion, which somewhat horrified me, that possibly a Parliament for Europe should be selected by the Whips. It would therefore be a Patronage Secretary's paradise, a sort of seraglio of eunuchs. Europe will not be served by such an institution. Without going further into the arguments put forward by the hon. Member for Gravesend, and while this matter is of extreme importance, it must be remembered that there are other topics which are of equal, if not greater, importance at the moment.

Mr Frank Bowles (Nuneaton): Before my hon. Friend leaves that point, I interrupted the speech of the right hon. Gentleman the Member for Orkney and Shetland (Mr Grimond) and said that the Lord Privy Seal had said: 'It will help to unite Europe in a barrier against Soviet Russia.' The Lord Privy Seal denied that. That was reported in the *Daily Express* on 13th October last.

Mr Foot: Perhaps what he said at the Conservative Party Conference was more candid than what he said here. He does have his candid moments.

I should have thought that most hon. Members would have come to the House since Parliament reassembled conscious of the fact that we face possibly the most dangerous international situation with which the world has ever been confronted. I can hardly say that the numbers attending the debates in the last two days provide convincing evidence that for the majority of hon. Members that is the case. We know why our numbers are not very great yesterday and today. The main reason is that the Opposition has not sought to put down an Amendment to the Gracious Speech relating to any question of defence and foreign policy. This is a deplorable state of affairs, for reasons I shall elaborate.

I should have thought that all hon. Members would consider that the international situation is one of extreme danger, partly because of the Russian explosions and partly because of some other events. I would have hoped that the Government would have made some attempt to analyse the international situation both in relation to the explosions of the Russian bombs, what happened at the 22nd Congress of the Communist Party in Russia, and in relation to all the other international events. We have not had such an analysis. Certainly we did not have it from the Lord Privy Seal today. Even less did we have it from the Prime Minister in his most deplorable speech two days ago. There has been no attempt whatever to examine what is happening in other parts of the world or to analyse the causes of the explosions. There was an attempt made by my hon. Friend the Member for Leeds, East (Mr Healey) today, and I believe that that was the first attempt to do so on the part of the Opposition Front Bench.

Most of the contributions to date have been politically illiterate, making no effort to relate what has happened to what has gone before or to the other developments that have occurred. Why has Russia exploded these bombs? I deplore and denounce the explosions, perhaps more than anyone and with more justification. Nevertheless we must see why they have happened. The Prime Minister says that it is a political act on the part of the Russians and that it had nothing to do with military measures. It was a terroristic act, he says, and that is the general claim made by most of the illiterate newspapers which make as little attempt to understand what is happening in the world as do the Government.

A terroristic act with no military significance, the explosions are called. One answer was given by my hon. Friend the Member for South Ayrshire (Mr Emrys Hughes) yesterday in his quotation from the *Economist*. It is perfectly possible that one military advantage of having a bigger bomb is that one can hit a Polaris weapon or that one would have a better chance of hitting it.

If that be true, then the bigger bomb has some military advantage. There was no attempt on the part of the Minister of Defence to answer the question. Instead, Government spokesmen continued their pretence that the only explanation they can discover is that it was some maniacal decision or act by Mr Khrushchev and the Russian leaders. But the Minister of Defence, curiously, a week or so ago repudiated or contradicted the explanation which the Prime Minister gave for the Russians exploding the bomb, or series of bombs. The Minister of Defence did not do it in his speech yesterday. It may be that he thought that it would be unseemly for him to repudiate the Prime Minister so quickly. He has the faculty which Lloyd George attributed to Stanley Baldwin of being able to stumble on a truth and then pick himself up as if nothing had happened.

On 24 October, when there were questions on a

statement by the Minister of Defence about the tests and the right hon. Gentleman was asked why he thought they had been made, he said: 'If one has to guess – and it can only be a guess – why the Russians have carried through this series of tests. I think that the best guess is that they have realised that they are behind the Americans in the development of nuclear weapons.' [*Official Report*, 24th October, 1961; Vol. 646, c. 752.] That seems to me a feasible explanation, but, if it is true, why go round talking about terrorist acts? Why go around saying that it is monstrously callous in a different sense from that in which the explosion of American bombs is callous? It appears to be the view of the Minister of Defence that the reason why the Russians have exploded these bombs is that they felt themselves inferior in nuclear power to the Americans. The Americans have told us, both before the last explosions and since, that they still possess overwhelmingly greater nuclear strength than the Russians. Is that true or not? If it is true that the Russians were greatly inferior in nuclear strength to the Americans, it may be that they have made the explosions to try to catch up with the Americans. If that is so, they are doing what the Americans and we do.

There are some of us in the House and many in the country – a growing number, as the Prime Minister recognised yesterday – who condemn all tests on humanitarian grounds. However, if the Minister of Defence's explanation of why the Russians have done it is correct, Her Majesty's Government have no grounds for complaining. The Russians are doing exactly what they did.

Mr Heath: Why did the Russians negotiate for more than two years on a test agreement, reject it at twenty-four hours' notice and then turn to tests? Why not carry out the tests underground instead of in the atmosphere where they are poisoning the air? Those are important questions.

Mr Foot: I shall deal with both of them. I should like there to be an agreement, but it happens to be the fact that the Americans had conducted many more explosions in the atmosphere than the Russians prior to these tests. I shall give the right hon. Gentleman the figures. If the right hon. Gentleman wishes to know why the Russians exploded their bombs in the atmosphere, one answer is – it is not my answer, but Mr Khrushchev's answer, which should be understandable to the right hon. Gentleman and to the Americans – that they are doing what the Americans did before.

Let me quote official estimates by the Americans included in the statement made in *The Times* on Monday from that newspaper's Washington correspondent quoting official statements made by the Government in Washington: 'An official estimate has it that the Soviet Union has now exploded a total of about 160 megatons compared with 130 megatons released by the United States, Britain and France. It states that the Soviet Union has deposited more radio-active debris in the atmosphere. The comparison given is that the radioactive fission product of all Soviet tests is about 7,328 lb compared with the Western total of 7,250 lb. The present series of Soviet tests is estimated to have generated 6,050 lb.' If that is correct, it means that the filth content, if I might translate these technical terms into simple language, was 7 to 1 – the Americans having contributed seven times as much filth as the Russians prior to this series of Russian tests, partly by explosions in the atmosphere. That, therefore, puts a rather different complexion on the matter.

When the Americans, together with the British and

French, were in the position of having poured seven times as much filth into the atmosphere as the Russians, many of us protested. We said that that was callous and inhuman and that it was poisoning the atmosphere. We still say it. However, the Government say it only when the Russians do it. How many protests did the Government make when the Americans had poured seven times as much filth into the atmosphere as the Russians? Not one. How can they expect anyone to believe them now?

If anyone believes in the balance of terror theory – I do not believe in it; I think that the balance of terror is much too precarious for anyone to put faith in it, and that it is a fallacy for people to put faith in it – the recent Russian explosions have restored the balance. East and West have exploded almost the same amount of megatons as each other. As I say, if anyone believes in the balance of terror, the Russians have been restoring it, and the Government must not complain too harshly when they restore it. The Government are not in a position to make such a protest.

In his reply to the question whether Britain was to continue with tests, the Prime Minister said that if we find ourselves in a position of military inferiority we shall have to go on with the tests, even those in the atmosphere. He said, as the Lord Privy Seal said, in effect, a minute or two ago, that they would try to confine them to underground tests, but he also said that if the Government found that in order to rectify a position of military inferiority it was necessary to carry out tests in the atmosphere, they would do so. Others have replied in similar terms. 'We know that it is impossible to beg for peace and tranquillity for the peoples . . . by preaching love and tolerance. We are compelled to answer military threats by strengthening our country's defence capacity. We have no other alternative.'

That is what the Government believe. But those are the words of Mr Khrushchev. When Mr Khrushchev protests about people exploding bombs in the atmosphere, I think that he is a hypocrite. But members of the Government Front Bench are hypocrites, too, because they do exactly the same thing.

The Lord Privy Seal referred to the way in which the Russians exploded their bombs. Although the explosion of the bombs is terrible enough in itself, in some respects the thing which contributed most to the unsettlement of the political atmosphere throughout the world, leaving aside the other atmosphere, was the timing and the way in which it was done. I agree with the right hon. Gentleman: I think that it is deplorable. It is interesting to try to discover why it should have happened. Surely those who want to discover what is happening in the world and how we can deal with it should consider the matter.

Mr Khrushchev made the statement a year or so ago which was quoted by the Leader of the Opposition a week or two ago condemning any possibility of anyone starting up tests and branding anyone who started up tests as someone who would be handed down to the shame of future generations, a quotation which he took from a newspaper called *Tribune*. We published it first. I am glad that my right hon. Friend has his copy delivered punctually. Clearly Mr Khrushchev was not intending to explode bombs then. It would have been too foolish. Therefore, at some point Mr Khrushchev thought that there was a possibility of reaching either a general test agreement or that it would not be necessary for the Soviet Union for any military reasons to go ahead with it. That is a feasible assumption.

Somehow or other, Mr Khrushchev and others changed their mind. It appears that Mr Khrushchev changed his mind fairly rapidly. There had been preparations for explosions before, but there have been preparations for explosions before in the United States, as the Lord Privy Seal knows. The fact that they made preparations for explosions while the test discussions were going on was not the worst crime. Both sides decided to make preparations to renew the tests.

What is the explanation? I do not know, and we can only guess, but I think that much the most intelligent guess that has been offered to the House so far has not come from the Government Benches and certainly not from the Leader of the Opposition either, but from my hon. Friend the Member for Leeds, East (Mr Healey) in the debate today. He sought to analyse what is happening in the Soviet Union – the fight against the anti-party group and between China and the Soviet leaders. That is nothing new. We should have known about this for years. We have known that something of the sort has been going on for years. It has not cropped up this month or last, and anybody studying these affairs could see after the death of Stalin that there has been a major discussion about policy continuing in the Soviet Union.

I remember the speech made by the right hon. Member for Woodford (Sir W. Churchill) in May, 1953, two or three months after the death of Stalin. It was much the most intelligent speech of any on this subject from the Conservative Benches, but it was never followed up. What the right hon. Gentleman said was that here there were great and profound changes obviously taking place in the Soviet Union, and that the major task of the British Government should be to explore these changes, to see how we could use them for the benefit of the world and our diplomacy. That was the appeal made by the right hon. Member for Woodford, but it was never followed up. The attempt of the right hon. Member for Woodford in 1953 to start negotiations with the Russians was destroyed by the other members of his Government. Instead, this country drove ahead as fast as we could with the plan for the rearmament of Germany.

I remember being told by my hon. Friend the Member for Leeds, East that if only we would rearm Germany discussions with the Russians would be much easier. The terrible feeling which I have about this situation is that we have missed our opportunities. If we look back, it was a merciful deliverance for the world, not only that Stalin died, as he was bound to die eventually, but when some people in the Soviet Union were prepared to try to change the whole course of Soviet policy. It was a merciful deliverance, and we should have aimed our policy, as a major objective, to try to encourage that development. We have done the exact opposite.

Mr Heath: I am following the hon. Gentleman's argument with the greatest interest, but surely he is wrong on this topic. Mr right hon. Friend the Member for Woodford put forward his proposals just before he ceased to be Prime Minister, and they were followed through by the present Earl of Avon in the Summit Conference of 1955. That was followed by a further Summit with my right hon. Friend the present Prime Minister taking part, and the Prime Minister himself went to Moscow two years ago to try to get negotiations going again, which was followed by the abortive Summit.

Mr Foot: I must bring the Lord Privy Seal up to date in his history. In fact, if he looks back, he will find that I am perfectly correct. After the right hon. Member for

Woodford had made his proposals for trying to seek an agreement or negotiations with the Russians in 1953, it was killed by Lord Salisbury and company. Everybody remembers the story. The right hon. Gentleman was still Patronage Secretary then, and perhaps did not follow these things closely, because we do not expect Patronage Secretaries to worry about the future of the world. The right hon. Gentleman now has higher responsibilities. I will come back to that point in a minute, and I will not forget it. It is a big jump from 1953 to 1959, but I will deal with what the Prime Minister said in 1959, when he went to Moscow, in a moment.

When one looks at this situation, I believe it is more desperate in some respects than ever before. What we wanted from the Government, and what I hoped we might have had in much clearer terms from the Opposition in this debate, was some attempt, not merely to curse the Russians for these abominations and explosions. I agree with denunciation if people would only curse these abominations by others as well.

We ought to have had the British Government putting forward a whole series of proposals to escape from the present dangerous situation. Some are very simple. Take the question of tests. Why do not the British Government give an absolutely clear declaration that we will never embark on any further nuclear tests? Why not? Instead of that, we have the statement of the Prime Minister, which was a mass of equivocations, and, as a result, we have a statement by the Washington correspondent of *The Times*, in describing the protests against the Russian explosion, saying that we are starting a move to resume tests. This is what the Washington correspondent said: 'Mr Macmillan's statement in the Commons yesterday is regarded as significant international support for a resumption' – that is, a resumption of tests. This is how the statement of the British Prime Minister is regarded in Washington. I think it is a most deplorable thing that a British Government do not try at this moment to resist any pressure to restart the tests and that we do not assist by saying that we shall never start any tests of our own. I am sorry that this matter has not been pressed strongly by the Opposition. After all, the Opposition are committed never to start these tests, and I do not see why they should not have put down a vote of censure on the Government about that, if they really mean it.

Let us take the question of some of the bases in this country – Thor missile bases. We were told by the Government yesterday that in August we were very near to mobilisation. The Government considered mobilising the Army and certain reservists to be sent to Germany. They decided not to do it, and I think they were very wise not to do it, but they came very near to it. It was a very serious situation, and, as one of my hon. Friends has said, if we had had a mobilisation of that nature it might have been considered as an act of war itself, and we might have been involved in a war. Yet, we have these Thor missiles here, and they are first strike weapons which can be used only as first strike weapons. Unless they are used as first strike weapons, they are useless.

The Leader of the Opposition has agreed previously that that was a perilous situation for this country. The peril of mobilisation made it worse. We might have had a situation building up suddenly about Berlin, when all the time we have these useless Thor weapons in Norfolk or wherever they are constituting magnets for attack, and, apparently, nobody in this country worried about it. In regard to the

Polaris weapon, the Government have not got control, do not decide whether they are to be used and whether they are to be fired. As the *Economist* said this week, it may be that one of the purposes of a much bigger megaton bomb is to deal with a weapon like Polaris. Yet this Government are so neglectful of the interests of the people of this country that they do not take any action about these matters. The Opposition are also committed by their conferences to be against the Thor missile and the Polaris missile, yet they do not do anything about it in votes of censure on that subject.

Take the question of the supply of nuclear weapons to Germany. A previous speaker from the Government side reported the feeling about nuclear weapons being supplied to Germany and also the feeling in Poland about the rearmament of Germany. As the hon. Member has just been to Poland, he knows what it is, and I can well imagine it, without having to go there. A week ago, the American Government signed a further agreement for the supply of nuclear weapons to the German forces. If the dangers of these weapons being let off are even only one-tenth as appalling as those described in the brilliant and devastating speech of my hon. and learned Friend the Member for Leicester, North-East (Sir L. Ungoed-Thomas) yesterday in regard to the danger of these tactical atomic weapons being let off – if the danger is only one-tenth of that which he described, then I think that having these dangerous weapons in the hands of American, British or other NATO troops is bad enough, but to put them into the hands of German troops is to take part in an act of provocation.

Yet the Government make no protests, the Opposition made hardly any protests, and it is the official policy of the Opposition to protest about it. I should have thought that to supply nuclear weapons to Germany was a perfectly sufficient ground for a vote of censure on the Government, because the Government permit these things to happen. Yet we have had no protest at all. They have agreed to provide Western Germany as part of NATO with these weapons, but they make no plans about any measures which ought to be taken to limit the dangers in an already explosive international situation.

My hon. Friend the Member for Leeds, East has already dealt with the matter, but I will say it again briefly. The Lord Privy Seal's answer this afternoon about proposals for a nuclear-free zone and disengagement in Europe were most disingenuous replies. He said that the time is not propitious. It never has been propitious as far as the Government are concerned, except at one moment in 1959 when the Prime Minister was in Moscow. He agreed to it being put in a communiqué, but otherwise has done nothing about it. He has abandoned it. He abandoned it almost as soon as he got back to this country. Yet the Leader of the Liberal Party was saying just now that he could not understand how people could look at the world today and place any blame on the Americans. According to his mythology, the Americans are the saints and the Russians are the devils. That is his liberal vision of the world scene.

How does the Leader of the Liberal Party explain the question of the Rapacki Plan? If a nuclear war does start we shall, in all probability, never find who was responsible for starting it. It will never be discovered. But even supposing that people could ransack all the books afterwards and discover how it started, what would they discover was the West's reply about the Rapacki Plan, a proposal put forward by the Polish Government in good faith and a proposal which could have kept the nuclear weapons out of the areas where they are at present and suggesting that these weapons should be removed from a larger territory in the East than in the West? These proposals were absolutely rejected by the American and British Governments.

The Lord Privy Seal cannot deny this. It is no good his saying that the moment is not propitious for these proposals. His Government have been adamantly opposed to them from the beginning. Why? Because the military chiefs say that they must pile these nuclear weapons into Germany and therefore will not begin to look at any plan for a nuclear-free zone. This is the real reason. In other words, the foreign policy of America, and therefore Great Britain, is governed by the decisions and the requirements, or the supposed requirements, of the military chiefs.

Coming back to the Leader of the Liberal Party, he is supporting the Western Powers which, on the major issue of a nuclear-free zone, have refused even to discuss what the Russians have proposed and what Mr Khrushchev proposed again only a few weeks ago. Moreover, the right hon. Gentleman is exonerating the West entirely when it is the West which is preventing negotiations on the most critical issue of the moment – Berlin.

I have been longer than I expected to be, but I was interrupted by the Lord Privy Seal. I was encouraging him to try to go further. In his speech the other day – I do not need to add much to what was said so well yesterday by my hon. Friend the Member for South Ayrshire – the Prime Minister said that although some of us on this side of the House represent a large number of people in the country we were pro-Russians and did not care for the name of England – we hated it. Well, I do not think that the Prime Minister is in a particularly good situation to question the patriotism of other hon. Members of the House. His career as Prime Minister started in the dishonour and deficit of Suez. He was responsible for introducing the White Paper in 1957–58 under which the British Government committed themselves to the most shameful proposition that any British Government has ever put forward, that we in certain circumstances would be the first to use the H-bomb. The right hon. Gentleman is responsible for that.

As was revealed from both sides of the House yesterday the Prime Minister has been responsible for leading us into the situation where we are more defenceless than ever before in our history. This is so on any test. Whether we take the test of those of us who are nuclear disarmers and who say that we cannot defend ourselves with nuclear weapons or whether we take the test of hon. Members opposite who say that we must have sufficient conventional weapons, this country is more defenceless than at any time in its history. This is not the time for a petulant and pathetic old man to come along and accuse other people – [Hon. Members: 'Shame.'] Yes, and even worse, if possible, than listening to the Prime Minister is the hardship we must suffer in listening to the statements of the Foreign Secretary – a kind of bellicose Bertie Wooster without even a Jeeves to restrain him.

We have a situation in which the world is in greater crisis than ever before, and yet the British Government have less to say than ever before on all the major issues of the day, less to say about tests, less to say about nuclear-free zones and less to say about how we can deal with the German problem. The British Government have abdicated. This is no time for the Government and the Prime Minister to come along and attack the patriotism of other hon. Members. Of course, the right hon. Gentleman complains that other people outside the House oppose the whole of the nuclear strategy, oppose it as a monstrous crime, for that is what it is. The Prime Minister thinks that it is wrong when the Russians engage in it but not wrong when anyone else engages in it.

I am glad to say that not only in this country but all over the world – we saw it again in the papers this morning – there are growing numbers of people who are protesting about the whole nuclear strategy whether adopted by the Americans, the British or the Russians. Mr Nehru said the other day – I wish that the statement could have been made by a British Prime Minister – that in two or three years' time India would have the power to make the bomb but was not going to do so. That is the kind of leadership which the world wants.

It is largely because instead of leadership we get in this House, not only from the Government but very often also from the Opposition Front Bench which refuses to put down Motions on the major issues of the day and refuses to challenge the Government on issues which matter even more than those on which they have put down Motions, complacency and hypocrisy that other people outside the House have to adopt other ways to make their protests. But they are going to continue their protests, and certainly the exhibition which we have had from the Prime Minister this week will encourage them to go on with their protests more strongly than ever.

Mr W. R. van Straubenzee (Wokingham): The House always fills with interest when the hon. Member for Ebbw Vale (Mr M. Foot) chooses to address it. It would not be proper for me to enter into the domestic controversy which the hon. Gentleman has sought to stir up on his own benches. As I was looking at him and listening to him I could not help thinking that his words and his gestures resembled one of the famous three witches of *Macbeth*, stirring their cauldron of trouble.

I am prepared to leave the hon. Gentleman to his task, but when he reads his speech tomorrow morning I doubt whether he will be as proud of it as he would have us believe. The argument behind the hon. Gentleman's mathematical statement is that in some extraordinary way because the filth released into the air by the Russian tests was mathematically equal to that released into the air by the American tests it made the Russian tests that little bit less reprehensible. This was a very clear inference in what the hon. Gentleman said and he must not be allowed to escape from it.

Appendix 3

Among the campaigners of the 1960s was one who put the argument against the deterrent in its full historical setting. For my money, no report on the scene would be proper which left Alan Taylor out. I reprint here the essay I wrote in one of the volumes of tribute to him.[1]

Alan Taylor, the teacher, must first be extolled; no one ever knew better how to stir the excitement of history. The great question – the word 'great', by the way, is one of his favourites which I eagerly purloin – is how he did it. I never attended those notorious, crowded morning lectures at Oxford when, without a note or a moment of hesitation or doubt, he would hold in the palm of his hand the whole audience, including a substantial proportion of the new historians in the rising generation. I did listen, with millions of others, when, against all the odds, this feat was repeated, word-perfect, theme-perfect, on the television screen. But before most others, I believe, I had the most exclusive showing, when for years on end, in the 1950s, we both appeared together almost every week on the same television show *In the News* on the BBC or *Free Speech* on ITV. Much the most thrilling part of those occasions was to hear Alan Taylor, the teacher, away from the cameras.

Over the years, he instructed us, first and foremost, on the greatness of the great historians. It was not so much that his choice was original; it wasn't. But he chose of course the great English narrative historians, and somehow he elbowed all the others out of the way into a lesser category. Number One, Macaulay: he could always say something new about Macaulay, and he was saying it again in one of his last diary pieces, written at the age of seventy-eight:

I have just read Macaulay's *History*, all five volumes of it. I am sometimes hailed as his successor ... I only wish I were. In my opinion he was the best narrative historian there has ever been, and I am proud to follow in his footsteps. I know that his consuming interest was in political affairs, which he understood from first-hand experience. Political history is frowned on nowadays except by me. But Macaulay was also the wittiest and most penetrating social historian when he wanted to be. He is one of the few historians who make the reader laugh. Gibbon also has his comic passages, but Gibbons's laughter is intellectual, Macaulay's is pure fun. Macaulay was often carried away by his own advocacy. Churchill alleged that he was a persistent liar, which is to get him all wrong. Macaulay was monstrously unfair to William Penn, though it is easy to see why. He was also dishonest in his dealing with Marlborough, but maybe that is less culpable than hero-worship. Indeed Macaulay's own hero-worship of William III is more at fault than his deni-gration of Marlborough. No one else would have ventured on the phrase William the Deliverer. Few historians now sing the praises of the Glorious Revolution. Here, I am on Macaulay's side. For me the Glorious Revolution remains the foundation of our liberty. All the more reason to praise it when the basic principles of parliamentary government are threatened as much from the Left as from the Right. However, this does not help my own problem: where am I to find intellectual and literary pleasure now that I have reached the final magical words, 'a lock of the hair of Mary'?

Let us return to Mary's lock and Alan's loving perception of it in a moment. Even granting Macaulay's pre-eminence, a few others, a very few, are not far behind. Gibbon himself, for example. In another mood or breath he will reinstate Gibbon as 'the greatest of English historians ... even though he hardly passes any of the present-day tests. He never looked at a single manuscript text. He did not know that the past is different from the present.' (Quite an indictment, for sure.) Yet Alan continued: 'He captures the reader with his wit rather than his scholarship, though that is pretty good as well.' How rare indeed that wit must have been to have made good for all other deficiencies. And so it was, allied with the will to tell the story in his own way, the indispensable Taylor requirement. And then the third of the great triumvirate, never to be displaced from their pedestals, Thomas Carlyle's *French Revolution*, 'the most powerful re-creation ever written'. Nothing but the most extreme superlative has a chance of proving suitable here, and always Alan would return to it: 'Carlyle sensed the masses as no other writer has done. He expressed their outlook against his own conscious convictions.'

But then again also I should recall that these private Te Deums were sung not only in praise of the safe and the established, even when, as always, he had his own peculiar reasons for allotting them their place in his Pantheon. He would guide us, even more eagerly, to some neglected masterpiece. I recall, for instance, how it was on his recommendation that I turned to Lady Gwendolen Cecil's *Life of Robert Marquis of Salisbury*, 'a work of art, a great biography', as Alan called it. It is indeed, and no one in his or her senses should ever miss it. But I still suspect Alan's motives. He was an admirer of Salisbury's foreign policy, and he detested Disraeli and all his works. I had dared to say a good word for Disraeli the novelist, not Disraeli the Tory leader and political mountebank. For Alan, this was going too far.

No good word about Disraeli should be tolerated in any circumstances; that was part of his Cobdenite, Gladstonian, Manchester School upbringing. However, even at this date, I must retort that the reference to Lady Gwendolen's work of art has a counter-productive effect. It showed how the old high Tory malice against the Jew-boy who saved them still rankled forty years after his death. Not to be missed, I assure you: no venom to equal the English aristocrat challenged in his own citadel.

However, leaving Gladstone and Disraeli aside for a moment, it was quickly apparent that we shared the same real heroes and that Alan could speak of them or write of them in a way no one had excelled before: for example, Thomas Paine: 'his *Rights of Man* is the greatest political disquisition written by an Englishman', or William Cobbett, 'the greatest Englishman', or at least the runner-up for the title (sometimes Alan puts forward Dr Johnson's claim for the title itself, but this unpardonable lapse must be forgotten), or Charles James Fox.

Reared in a true liberal home and captivated at an early age by Trevelyan's classic *Early History of Charles James Fox*, I was naturally outraged by the scurvy Namier denigration of Fox and comparably encouraged when so flaming a radical as Alan rallied to his defence. Almost always in those early tutorial classes in which he gave me private inspiration, we were on the same side, and our differences were rare and insignificant. I did sometimes wonder why he would accord such honour to Cobden and Bright, and then withhold it from the Chartist leaders who seemed to me greater men still, made from a different mould. I had an occasional, daring suspicion: would not Feargus O'Connor and William Lovett or Julian Harney have been given their due from Alan more readily if they had come from the north, had been born in Manchester, Salford or even Southport? Cobden and Bright and Alan Taylor were splendid theoretical internationalists; but they would insist on speaking in a strong Lancashire accent.

Sometimes too those behind-the-scenes disputations would turn to the lofty question: what is history? And here, as all his pupils know, Alan's invective was more powerful than ever. He could denounce the historical system-makers, Toynbeeism, Burkhardtism, Actonism and every other ism almost with a special, splendid scorn. But what of Marxism? He once called himself a Marxist, and the Marxists, at least the most intelligent of them such as E. J. Hobsbawm, always treated him in turn with a wary, critical reverence. He never attempted to disguise his adoration for the *Communist Manifesto* and *The Eighteenth Brumaire of Louis Napoleon*, while the materialist conception of history could still be treated as a Toynbeeite absurdity. He was the sworn enemy of every theory but his own, yet he always retained a short sharp answer to the inscrutable question. History, he wrote (in what he called his favourite book), 'is distinguished from social studies by the fact that in it things happen one after another'.

No bones could be barer, could they? Not a speck of flesh anywhere. Facts, facts, facts. Reality stripped of all sentiment, sentences without verbs; slap them down on the table, like a card player with a fistful of trumps. And never suppose that politicians apply principles, plans, systems, ideologies. Only Taylor's fellow historians are fat-headed enough to imagine that. Oh no! The leaders of men, the best and the worst, live from hand to mouth, from hour to hour, pursue nothing but their own noses, and the people follow, usually with much too much obedience. Such was the Taylor non-theory, which he illustrated afresh, for instance, and magnificently in a spectacular television series called *The War Lords*. We learnt how Hitler stumbled into war; how Stalin stumbled to victory; how Roosevelt picked his way by the most devious means to his liberal pedestal from which the liberal realists so fatuously sought to dislodge him; how Churchill, having achieved power on the ashes of his own Churchill-contrived Norwegian fiasco, stumbled thereafter with the best and the worst, snatching victories from defeats, and defeats from victories.

Let us acknowledge at once: the Taylor non-theory offers many attractions in practice. Taylorite originality is inexhaustible and unfailing. At his best he was always searching for the muddled, inconvenient, disconcerting truth, and stating it in succinct, down-to-earth language. The language indeed is very much part of the man; the staccato style bullies the reader into submission, as if he were perpetually having a pistol stuck in his ribs. And these qualities of simplicity and directness, Alan implies, are the necessary talents for a historian. He once called this his Bren-gun style, and said he got it from Macaulay.

Alas, most of his fellow historians, or at least those who had the disposition of academic offices at their command, never saw matters in this light. Right from his earliest academic days he showed a marvellous ability to fill Oxford lecture rooms at breakfast time and seduce young minds away from the chaste rut of orthodoxy. He gave them history lessons they had never heard before, and his fellow dons shook their heads gravely. Then he became a television star, and wrote scandalous and highly paid articles for Sunday newspapers, and they shook their heads more gravely than ever. The result was that the most popular of modern historians, truly the Macaulay of this century, was never recognised in his own university.

The first Alan Taylor book I read displayed these qualities in a peculiar setting. It was called *The Struggle for Mastery in Europe 1848–1914*, and dealt with established opinions in just about the best documented period in our history. I started to read it in the belief that even Taylor would have to control his iconoclasm as he marched along those well-beaten tracks. But within a few pages it was evident that all orthodoxies, including Socialist orthodoxies, were to be overturned. That was supposed to be the era *par excellence* of imperialism, when the quest for markets in Asia and Africa transformed the contest in Europe. That was the age which H. N. Brailsford had described in his *The War of Steel and Gold: A Study of the Armed Peace*. That was the age which J. A. Hobson had forecast in his prophetic book on imperialism, which even Lenin himself had adapted for his world-shattering designs. But along came Taylor and knocked all those theories through the ropes. He showed, with staggering simplicity, how the statesmen before 1914 kept their eye on the ball – on the balance of power on the European continent. They did then what statesmen did again in the 1960s and thereafter. They pursued power for its own sake, failed to define coherently their own purposes, chased their own tails. Strategy, not economics, governed diplomacy.

The Introduction to that same 'old-fashioned' diplomatic history, by the way, contained a few paragraphs which illustrated the Taylor genius at its peak, the combination of breath-taking generalisation worthy of Marx himself with detailed incidents, worthy, shall we say, of Pepys, another of Alan's unlikely heroes: 'In the last resort the First World War was brought about by the coincidence of two opposite beliefs. The rulers of Austria-Hungary believed that there would be revolution if they did not launch a war; the rulers of Germany were confident that there would not be a revolution if they did.' 'Both beliefs', added Taylor, 'would have astonished Metternich.' And when Victor Adler objected to Berchtold, foreign minister of Austria-Hungary, that war would provoke revolution in Russia, even if not in the Hapsburg monarchy, he replied: '"And who will lead this revolution? Perhaps Mr Bronstein sitting over there at the Cafe Central?"' Mr Bronstein was, of course, Leon Trotsky, and thus Alan Taylor, the anti-theory historian, quoted an historical accident to upset the theorists.

And perhaps this is the moment to take that fresh, promised glance at the lock of hair. Macaulay made a hero out of the William III whom modern scholars have reduced to the status of a dour, calculating homosexual. Such a demotion is impossible to believe when one reads the last few pages of Macaulay's history, when the king was dying, which do indeed reveal how short, sharp sentences, every one immediately, palpably intelligible, can produce the effect, and 'when the most rigid Pharisee of the Society for the Reformation of Manners could hardly deny that it was lawful to save the state, even on the Sabbath . . . He closed his eyes, and gasped for breath. The bishops knelt down and read the commendatory prayer. When it ended William was no more. When his remains were laid out, it was found that he wore next to his skin a small piece of black silk riband. The lords in waiting ordered it to be taken off. It contained a gold ring and a lock of the hair of Mary.'

Every Taylor book, fat or slim, contains a wealth of similar treasures. I can count some twenty or thirty of them on my shelves, produced while his honour-laden competitors have been content with much more meagre tomes. I have picked out one at random. It is *The Trouble Makers*, and I see that Alan has written his own judgement in it for me: 'My best book.' I opened it again at random and read on page 100: 'It was no mean achievement for Hobson [the J. A. Hobson quoted above] to anticipate Keynesian economics with one flick of the wrist and to lay the foundations for Soviet policy with another. No wonder that he never received academic acknowledgement nor held a university chair.'

I turned over the pages again with endless curiosity and fascination. 'Today's realism will appear tomorrow as short-sighted blundering. Today's idealism is the realism of the future.' And if you are reaching for a pinch of salt, to couple with that dose of not-so-frequent Taylorite Socialist dreaming, let me tell you that what he offers on page after page is something approaching *proof*, and patriotic proof at that. 'The dissenters', Taylor insists,

> have been deeply English in blood and temperament – often far more so than their respectable critics. Paine, Cobbett, Bright, Hobson, Trevelyan – what names could be more redolent of our English past? One of the dissenters found better words than mine: 'How indeed, can I, any more than any of you, be un-English and anti-national? Was I not born upon the same soil? Do I not come of the same English stock? Are not my family committed irrevocably to the fortunes of this country? Is not whatever property I may have depending as much as yours is depending upon the good government of our common fatherland? Then how shall any man dare to say to one of his countrymen, because he happens to hold a different opinion on questions of great public policy, that therefore he is un-English, and is to be condemned as anti-national?'

Alan would describe how he recited those words with peculiar affection. The first advice on European history he was given on arrival at Oxford University was to read that speech of John Bright. Bright was one in Alan Taylor's gallery of Manchester heroes, but Richard Cobden was the favourite. Often, as I have indicated before, I would challenge Alan on his allegiance to these bourgeois figures; why would he not accord his accolade to the Chartists? Surely they were even more deserving of Socialist sustenance than this middle-class Manchester crew, but he would have none of it. Richard Cobden remained for him the most immaculate of great men. My impression is that his prejudice was influenced not solely by Cobden's Manchester connection, but also by the manner in which he argued. 'Our political past', he wrote, again in that book *The Trouble Makers*, 'was shaped by the clash of argument as well as by family connections and systems of land tenure.' This was a sentence primarily designed to dismiss the Namiers and the Trevor-Ropers. It also serves the purpose of indicating why history, as told by Taylor, retained its perpetual modern inflection. While pretending to search only for the facts, he was also looking for the ideas and the arguments, in nooks and crannies, where most of the orthodox historians were never inquisitive enough to poke their noses. And that, perhaps, is the way in which he established his famous or infamous friendship with Lord Beaverbrook.

Taylor read Beaverbrook's books on politics with fresh eyes. The style, in any case, had a kinship with his own; the taste of the two men for brevity and clarity was similar. But Taylor also set aside the preconceived assumption that Beaverbrook must be a second-rate journalist writing for the hour or the day or for the immediate sensation. He wrote a review in the *Observer* in which, incredibly in the light of all previous academic judgements, he compared Beaverbrook with Tacitus.

I was present in the room when Beaverbrook read that

review, and his life was transformed. He had indeed always been most modest about his own writings, never expecting to be regarded as anything more than a chronicler, the good teller of a tale which he knew himself to be and had every right to accept as a fair assessment. As for the comparison with Tacitus, utterly flattering as he believed it to be, it meant that a new world and a new friendship had opened before him. Alan Taylor became his intimate confidant on all these questions, his biographer, and perhaps his truest friend. Certainly the public judgement on Beaverbrook's writings was transformed by that single verdict. Not all his writings, of course, are in any sense in the same class. Most of them *were* sheer journalism. But the three or four main books on politics *are* masterpieces of political writing, and it took Alan Taylor's discernment – and his courage – to make the discovery in full measure.

Few of his other fellow historians are ever treated with such sympathy; instead, they are more often the victims of the Taylor contrariness. He upsets every orthodox apple-cart in sight and fouls his own academic nest with aquiline droppings. To change the metaphor hastily, his whole performance resembles more a Guy Fawkes night in which rockets, squibs, Catherine wheels and Roman candles crackle and flare in endless profusion.

Carlyle himself once said: 'How inferior for *seeing* with is your brightest train of fireworks to the humble farthing candle.' True, no doubt, but fortunately Carlyle never felt it necessary to abide by his own precept, and fortunately too Alan Taylor has never suffered from these pious inhibitions. Both loved paradox; both knew the art of overstatement. What Macaulay and Carlyle and Taylor all had in common, and the reason why they are great narrative historians, is that they are ready to risk making judgements in every paragraph, almost every sentence. They write with simple, reckless passion, like poets or pamphleteers. It is not an easy style to acquire, which is why so few survive from one century to another. Study those Taylor epigrams and paragraphs more carefully, and one can see how elaborate their interlocking architecture may be; how he had devised for himself a style which could be turned to every purpose and would never lose its appeal. The reader's attention is never lost for a single second. Such a purpose could never have been pursued if it had not been serious. And, of course, he was at his most serious in facing the greatest peril for all mankind.

He knew more about the cause of the two world wars of this century than anyone else on the planet. This did not mean that we must accept as irrefutable his explanation of the likeliest cause of the Third World War. But at least his opinion should not be just pushed aside. He knew much more about the whole subject than, say – to put the claim as modestly as possible – the Secretary of State for Defence, at the time he was writing [his autobiography], a Mr Michael Heseltine.

Alan Taylor had expounded his view on these matters in defiance of orthodox opinion and, more especially, left-wing orthodox opinion. He showed how the origins of the First World War were to be traced much more to upsets of the balance of power in Europe than to the struggle for markets in Africa. He brought fury on his head from all quarters, Left, Right and Centre, when some thirty years after most experts had pronounced all debate about the origins of the Second World War dead and buried, he carried out a brilliantly successful exhumation.

In some respects, particularly in its timing, the volume which caused all the trouble on this occasion – *The Origins of the Second World War* – was the bravest or, if you wish, the most reckless he ever wrote. His purpose was to apply the Taylor doctrine or non-doctrine of history to the 1930s, to Hitler and his opponents and his appeasers, to illustrate how accidents, miscalculations, short-term expectations could produce the mightiest convulsions, how all men, even power-crazed dictators, could never impose their rigid wills according to some fancied destiny; much more probably they too would be caught in traps which they had never envisaged. Of course, his aim was not to exonerate Hitler, to excuse those who had fawned on him, although he did declare his wish to restore some of its ancient credit to the old word *appeasement*. The manner of his statement was not in the fashionable idiom of the time (the one which had become fashionable only after 1939 or even 1940). He looked at this historical period, as he did at all others, as one in which the choices were still open. Even the Hitler war could have been avoided if other possibilities had been explored, by the politicians and nations who should have been ranged against the dictators, no less than the dictators themselves. It was a brave and brilliant attempt to tell the truth.

But his enemies pounced from all sides. Some jaundiced academic authorities had been waiting to catch him in the coils of his own paradoxes. Political opponents had even stronger incentives. Just at that moment he was at the peak of his notoriety as a leading campaigner for nuclear disarmament, and had he not exposed himself in his true colours as a lily-livered appeaser, the only man who dared utter the dirtiest word in the political dictionary? How they all set upon him, led by his old sparring partner who had beaten him to the Oxford history chair, Hugh Trevor-Roper – not yet disguised as a Cambridge Head of College, a Conservative Peer of the Realm and our chief exposer of Hitler forgeries, a more profitable vein in Sunday journalism than Alan had ever dared to open!

It was the moment when Alan showed most intrepidly his combined devotion to his political faith and his craft as a historian. Others might have been crushed by such an assault, but how little his assailants knew their man. In pursuit of historical truth, the old Cobdenite had been ready to pay proper honour to Palmerston. And nothing then or thereafter would prevent him from uttering, in language so simple that everyone could understand, what new crimes the human race might be contemplating, and who might be the criminals, and his knowledge of history should teach us all not to confuse the lessons of different epochs, not to debase for ever such honourable words as appeasement, not to imagine so cosily that the challenge of world-wide extermination had ever been presented in the same form before. He expressed some of these truths more simply than anyone else. Perhaps that was his real offence; the people *could* understand. Thomas Paine had once been found guilty of high treason for the same reason.

So what did that brave voice, quite accustomed to the wilderness for a platform, say about our present predicament and our future? He said it most bluntly in his Romanes Lecture for 1981. The sentences are uttered with Macaulayesque assurance, Johnsonian finality: 'The prime cause of the war lay in the precautions that had been taken to ensure that there would be no war. The deterrent dominated strategical planning before 1914. The deterrent did not prevent war: it made war inevitable.' Then, later, he concluded, rising to an unscripted, inspired climax:

> I deplore the historians who, against all past experience, declare that this time the deterrent in the shape of nuclear weapons will preserve peace for ever. The deterrent starts

off only as a threat, but the record shows that there comes a time when its reality has to be demonstrated – which can only be done by using it. So it was in August 1914 and so it will be again. So far we have done very well. We have lived under nuclear terror for forty years and are still here. The danger increases every day. Without the abolition of nuclear weapons the fate of mankind is certain.

Can nothing be done to avert this fate? We can expect nothing from the nuclear scientists, the political experts, and, least of all, the statesmen. But for ordinary people there still remain standards of right and wrong. One of these is that no country, no political system, is entitled to employ mass murder in order to maintain itself. We are often told that the renunciation of nuclear weapons by a single country – I hope our country – would expose it to nuclear destruction once it could not retaliate. I believe that the reverse is the truth: if we do not possess nuclear weapons there is no point in destroying us. In any case, is it not morally better to face, perhaps to experience, nuclear obliteration than to inflict this obliteration on others?

These weapons of mass destruction are designed and manufactured by human beings. Politicians and military leaders may initiate the preparations for nuclear warfare but the actual manufacture is in the hands of scientists whose devotion should be to the future of mankind. For that matter, every citizen of a free country has a responsibility to help in ridding the world of nuclear weapons. This will not be easy, but it must be done.

This was the note of warning which, in our most perilous age, made Alan's voice more effective than any other. The philosophers led by Bertrand Russell, the writers led by J. B. Priestley, the scientists led by Solly Zuckerman, the journalists led by James Cameron, the astronomers led by Martin Ryle, the churchmen too, as we atheists must acknowledge, led by Donald Soper and Canon Collins and

Bruce Kent, all put their case for nuclear disarmament with great force. No one did it with stronger authority than Alan Taylor; no one has answered his Romanes Lecture.

One reason why he did it so effectively derives from another quality which so far I have not attempted to indicate in these pages. Despite all his own assertions to the contrary, he has a theme, a flag to wag, a sentimental cause, a hero, apart even from Cobden. He is a great little Englander, and at the end of his own book on England he typically squeezed a purple passage into an aphorism: 'The British Empire declined; the condition of the people improved. Few now sang "Land of Hope and Glory". Few even sang "England Arise!" England has risen, all the same.'

That tribute was provoked by the conduct of the British people – his English, with the others allowed in to share the glory – in the war of 1939–45. And Taylor loved the facts and the English, and, for all his aggressive scepticism, he could never quite disentangle one from the other. The peace-loving Cobdenite believed it was abundantly right to fight and win the most legitimate war in history, right for the English people he loved, and right for the democratic Socialist cause in which he had always set his faith. All the more did he deserve an audience when he told us that the new weapons transformed the scene and that deterrence would not work any more than it did before.

Curiously, the Alan Taylor who was often taunted for his cynicism, who prided himself on his realism, returned to his old Dissenter's doctrine: 'Conformity may give you a quiet life; it may even bring you a University Chair. But all change in history, all advance comes from nonconformity. If there had been no trouble-makers, no Dissenters, we should still be living in caves.'

And what was the Dissenters' chosen weapon?

It is a question of morals. Sooner or later we shall have to win the younger generation back to morality. I wonder where they learnt that it was buncombe. Was it from contemporary philosophers or from the day-to-day behaviour of statesmen? This country of ours fought two world wars mainly for high principle; and the only lesson drawn from this by the young is that might is right. It now seems unbearably priggish to say that the country which went to war for the sake of Belgium and Poland must not, in any circumstances, drop the H-bomb. But it is true.

Notes

Preface

1 Suzanne Goldenberg, *Guardian*, 17 June 1998.
2 James Cameron, *An Indian Summer* (Newton Abbot, Readers' Union, 1959).
3 Charles Moran, *Winston Churchill: The Struggle for Survival 1940–1965* (London, Sphere, 1968), pp. 503–12.
4 *Hansard*, House of Commons, 2 March 1955, vol. 537, cols 2109–22.
5 Moran, *Struggle for Survival*, pp. 439–40.
6 H. G. Wells, *The World Set Free* (London, Collins, 1914; new edn Hogarth, 1988), pp. 73–4.
7 Ibid, pp. 95–6.
8 Lord Byron, 'Darkness', *Byron* (Oxford Authors), ed. Jerome J. McGann (Oxford, Oxford University Press, 1986), pp. 272–3.

Chapter 1

1 See Dwight David Eisenhower, *Waging Peace: 1956–1961* (London, Heinemann, 1966), p. 494.
2 Jawaharlal Nehru, *The Unity of India: Collected Writing, 1937–1940* (London, Lindsay Drummond, 1942), pp. 220–40.
3 Dwight Eisenhower, farewell address as President of the United States, 17 January 1961.
4 The tape transcripts were published as Ernest R. May and Philip D. Zelikow, eds, *The Kennedy Tapes* (Cambridge, Mass., Belknap, 1997).
5 Quoted in Edward Luttwak, *Times Literary Supplement*, 6 February 1998.
6 Harold Macmillan, *At the End of the Day* (London, Macmillan, 1973), pp. 181–220.
7 Indira Gandhi, speech to parliament after Simla agreement: Pupul Jayakar, *Indira Gandhi* (London, Viking, 1988), p. 251. See also <http://pak.gov.pk/govt/kashmir/kashmir-simla.htm>.

8 Comment on India nuclear test of May 1974: Natwar Singh, *Profiles and Letters* (London, Sangam Books, 1998), p. 181.

9 Bhutto, comment at press conference, Lahore, May 1974, *The Times of India*, 19 May 1974.

10 A brilliant study of these matters is offered in Rafi Raza's *Sulfikar Ali Bhutto and Pakistan 1957–1977* (Oxford, Oxford University Press, 1998). Raza was a supporter of Bhutto who observed him in action through thick and thin. Bhutto came to believe that the Americans turned on him in the end partly because of his overblown rhetoric about the 'Islamic bomb'. Maybe; the author is even more critical than his leader of US arrogance and the way in which the Americans could wield their influence so banefully behind the scenes; he could squirm when he saw Bhutto ingratiating himself with Kissinger.

11 Bhutto's 'eat grass' quote became even more famous than his anti-American outbursts.

Chapter 2

1 Bertrand Russell, *Common Sense and Nuclear Warfare* (London, Allen & Unwin, 1959), p. 1.

2 Michael Foot, *CND News*, August 1964.

3 Quoted in Lawrence S. Wittner, *Resisting the Bomb: The World Disarmament Movement 1954–1970*, vol. 2: *The Struggle Against the Bomb* (Stanford, Stanford University Press, 1997), pp. 121–3.

4 S. Zuckerman, *Nuclear Illusion and Reality* (London, Collins, 1982).

5 Earl Mountbatten, 'Nuclear Arms Race has no Military Purpose', 1979.

6 Robert McNamara described the futility and the danger of this whole cruise missile/SS-20s episode of the early 1980s in his first book on the subject, happily named *Blundering into Disaster* (London, Bloomsbury, 1987) pp. 74–5. The installation of the missiles in various European countries, including Britain, was supposed to give confidence that they would not be picked off severally by attacks from the Soviet Union. The fallacy in the argument was that the decision to use any of the weapons still rested absolutely with the President of the United States. So several intelligent Western leaders came to the conclusion we would be safer without

them – like the brave women of Greenham Common who gave the lead in this matter.

7 *Hansard*, House of Lords, 16 February 1983, vol. 439, cols 253–7.
8 McNamara's book *Blundering into Disaster* also exposed the claims that somehow the Soviet Union had been allowed to forge ahead in the nuclear race. All the real evidence pointed to an exactly opposite conclusion.
9 Russell, *Common Sense and Nuclear Warfare*, appendix.
10 Indira Gandhi, Belgrade, 1980; see Pupul Jayakar, *Indira Gandhi* (London, Viking, 1988).
11 Philip Morrison on nuclear winter, ibid., p. 458.
12 Sunil Khilnani, *The Idea of India* (London, Hamish Hamilton, 1997).

Chapter 3

1 Mikhail Gorbachev, *Memoirs* (New York and London, Doubleday, 1996).
2 Mikhail Gorbachev, *Perestroika* (London, Collins, 1987), p. 226.
3 Gorbachev, *Memoirs*, pp. 414–20.

Chapter 4

1 P. V. Narasimha Rao at non-aligned summit, 18–20 October 1995, *India Abroad*, 2 February 1996; more details at <http://www.nonaligned.org>.
2 Arundhati Ghose, United Nations Standing Conference on Disarmament at Geneva, 1996: *India Abroad*, 2 February 1996; see <http://www.unorg.ch/genet/disarm/disarmconf.htm>.
3 Seema Mustafa, *The Asian Age*, April 1998.
4 Ibid.
5 Ibid.
6 Seema Mustafa, *The Asian Age*, 16 May 1998.
7 Comment on Israeli overflight of Chaghi Hills; *The Asian Age*, 25 May 1998.
8 M. J. Akbar, *The Asian Age*, 1 June 1998.
9 Ibid.
10 Ibid.
11 Report of National Conference, Srinagar, 8 June 1998, *The Asian Age*.

12 Sukumar Muralidharan, *Frontline*, 14 August 1998.
13 Arundhati Roy, 'The End of Imagination', *Frontline*, August 1998; this can be read at <http://www.outlookindia.com/previous/3aug/features/htm>.

Chapter 5

  1 UK *Strategic Defence Review*, presented to Parliament 8 July 1998; can be read at <http://www.mod.uk/policy/sdr/index.htm>.
  2 If the description of President Clinton's conduct in that August as midsummer madness is seen as too severe, we may note that the whole question of new routes to old poisons was authoritatively reviewed by Owen Bowcott in the *Guardian*, 4 November 1998. His report on the perils of the new kind of gases was indeed legitimately alarming. But he reported also on the basis of American evidence that Clinton had acted on 'gossamer-thin evidence'. Every further examination of the event confirmed that the President had no real justification for his action, and that those who believed him were fools. The more serious the threat from the new poisons is taken to be, the more indefensible the President's choice of retaliatory action.
  3 Richard Norton-Taylor, *Guardian*, 8 September 1998.
  4 Claudia McElroy, *Guardian*, 19 March 1998.
  5 *Observer*, 11 October 1998.
  6 *The Asian Age*, 1 May 1998, commenting on Lachlan Forrow et al., 'Accidental Nuclear War: A Post-Cold War Assessment', Special Report, *The New England Journal of Medicine*, 30 April 1998, vol. 338, no. 18. Copies can be ordered from <http://www.nejm.org>.
  7 K. Subrahmanyam, 'Bomb in a Box: A Clear and Present Danger', *The Times of India*, 1 December 1997.
  8 Robin Cook, 'Bombs Away', *New Statesman and Society*, 12 April 1995.
  9 Declaration of Non-Aligned Movement, 5 September 1998.
10 Ed Vulliamy, *Guardian*, 19 August 1998.
11 Robert McNamara, *In Retrospect: The Tragedy and Lessons of Vietnam* (New York, Times Books, 1995).
12 Ibid., p. 285.

13 Ursula Fanthorpe, *Safe as Houses* (Calstock, Cornwall, Peterloo Books, 1995).

Appendix 2

1 *Hansard*, House of Commons, 2 November 1961, vol. 628, cols 382–95.

Appendix 3

1 *Warfare, Diplomacy and Politics: Essays in Honour of A. J. P. Taylor* (London, Hamish Hamilton, 1986).

Index